Building the Write Life

Also by Richard Estep

In Search of the Paranormal
Haunted Longmont
The World's Most Haunted Hospitals
Trail of Terror
Colorado UFOs
The Devil's Coming to Get Me
The Fairfield Haunting
Haunted Healthcare
Haunted Healthcare 2
The Black Monk of Pontefract
The Horrors of Fox Hollow Farm
The Dead Below

As co-author

The Haunting of Asylum 49
Spirits of the Cage

Building the Write Life

How *You* Can Make it as a Published Author

Richard Estep

Copyright 2019 Richard Estep

All rights reserved

For Autumn

8/9/98 – 7/19/19

We miss you.

Clear skies.

Contents

Introduction
Chapter 1 – What to Write
Chapter 2 – Genre, and the Art of Writing to Market
Chapter 3 – Getting it Written
Chapter 4 – Where do I Start?
Chapter 5 – Where am I Going?
Chapter 6 – Your Daily Word Count
Chapter 7 – Jedi Mind Tricks
Chapter 8 – Resistance
Chapter 9 – The Edit
Chapter 10 – Test Readers
Chapter 11 – Choose Your Path
Chapter 12 – Traditional Publishing
Chapter 13 – Self (Indie) Publishing
Chapter 14 – The Hybrid Author
Chapter 15 – Road Map: Traditional Publishing
Chapter 16 – Road Map: Indie Publishing
Chapter 17 – Marketing and Branding
Chapter 18 – A Larger World
Chapter 19 – Your Writing Journey
Acknowledgments

Introduction

The Write Life

Writing, publishing, and getting paid for the privilege of having others read what you have written, is one of the most exhilarating, satisfying, and terrifying roller coasters you'll ever get to ride in your life.

It's also immensely frustrating. Or, as they like to say in my native Great Britain, a right royal pain in the arse (that's *ass*, for my American friends).

It can be a lonely thing sometimes, this business of sitting down at the keyboard and staring at a blank white screen, waiting for inspiration to strike...waiting for the words to come. Nobody else can do it for you. Not me. Not your loved ones. Not one of the countless self-help and how-to books for writers that fill the market, of which this is just one.

No. Only *you* can do it. Your ultimate success — or failure — is all down to you, and you alone.

And that's scary. Understandably so. It's why so many people start out full of optimism, writing in a blaze of nervous energy, hammering out what they believe will be their magnum opus…only to get bogged down in the mire of uncertainty (usually somewhere in the middle of their book) and, when optimism turns into frustration, abandon the whole damn thing and start something else…or, even worse, wave goodbye to their dreams of being a writer and move on to something else. The next big thing in their life.

Something easier.

Maybe you've done that yourself. If you have, there's no shame in it. In fact, you're in good company. I've heard from more people than I can count, usually those who approach me at a book signing or convention. Almost all of them have the air of somebody who feels as though they have good reason to be embarrassed.

"I've always wanted to write my own book," they'll often say, with just a trace of nervousness and self-deprecation. Sometimes it's a case of: "I started writing, but it never really went anywhere."

All of which makes me wonder just how many beautiful stories, whether fiction or non-fiction (it really doesn't matter) are floating around out there unfinished, simply abandoned and lost in the ether. How many tales are going untold, just because their tellers are either unable to complete them, or are unsure of how to get them published?

If you're one of those aspiring writers, then this book is meant for you. My goal in writing it has been a simple one: to help you get across the finish line, to reach that pair of magical words — *The End* — that signify the end of the race.

But that's not all.

Once your book is finished, it needs to be hammered into shape. That means revising, rewriting, editing, editing, and still more editing. Then, and only then, do you have a shot at getting it published, and — let's not downplay the importance of this next part — making you a little money too.

I hate to sound mercenary about this, but I've always found the notion of the so-called 'starving artist' to be more ridiculous than romantic. Now, don't get me wrong: if your sole purpose for writing is to have a good time, banging out a few hundred words here and there, without a care as to what happens to the finished product, then knock yourself out. More power to you. In fact, there's a long-standing tradition of purely recreational writing, of storytelling simply for the sake of it; the pure, unadulterated joy of the creative process. If this kind of writing is your thing, my hat goes off to you. Long may you derive joy from expressing your creativity in this way.

But I didn't write this book for you.

I wrote this book for someone who aspires to be a professional writer, somebody who wants to not only see their words printed, but also bound (or digitally formatted) and put into the hands of a reader.

These are the writers who are reaping the financial dividends of their hard work and talent.

Talent. That's rather a loaded term, isn't it? How arrogant would it be to apply that word to yourself — to think of yourself as a *talented* writer?

I used to think about that over and over again. I wasn't *talented*, I would tell myself. My writing was passable, sure, or at the very best proficient…but was I talented? Oh, *hell no.*

Just who did I think I was?

As things turned out, this was false modesty at its worst.

How do I know this?

Because no less an authority than Stephen King said so, and who am I to argue with Stephen King?

If you wrote something for which someone sent you a check, Mr. King said, *if you cashed the check and it didn't bounce, and if you then paid the light bill with the money, I consider you talented.*

(You can find the original interview at *https://www.aerogrammestudio.com/2015/02/24/stephen-king-everything-you-need-to-know-about-writing-successfully/*)

Flash back to 2015. I had just received a contract from an honest-to-goodness, real-world publishing house for my first book, *In Search of the Paranormal: The Hammer House Murder, Ghosts of the Clink, and other Disturbing Cases.*

The publisher sent me a small advance, with the promise of another one once the 55,000-word manuscript was delivered, accepted, and signed off on by their editor.

"Holy crap, I'm a writer," I kept repeating to myself, over and over again. I stood in the kitchen and held the check up to the light, staring at the watermark and trying to convince myself that my lifelong dream really had just become a reality at long last.

I was a professional writer, and not only that, according to the world's acknowledged grand master of horror fiction, I was a *talented* writer as well.

The next day, I banked the check and spent the money. I can't remember what I spent it on, but it almost certainly wasn't the light bill. That would have been just a little *too* perfect, wouldn't it?

That kind of thing only happens in stories.

Stories. We'll get to those later.

The Dream

There's an old saying which goes something like this: *"Everybody's got at least one book in them."*

But is it true? Many people don't think so. Not everybody is cut out to be a writer, they say, in much the same way that not everybody is cut out to be a nurse, a teacher, a husband, a parent, a marathon runner…or any one of a million different labels that people like to apply to themselves, and to one another.

Oh, anybody can *write*; the chances are that you do it every day, most often in the form of emails and texts. But that's not '*proper*' writing…

…is it?

Let's take a closer look at what it means to be a writer. The word is really an umbrella term, one which encompasses a vast spectrum of possibilities. For the sake of clarity, I'm going to focus primarily on those aspects which involve making a paycheck of some sort or another.

If you write a 2,000-word article about serial killers, let's say, and manage to get it published in an online magazine or journal, then you're a writer.

If you write a 60,000-word non-fiction book about things that go bump in the night, one which sits on the shelves of bookstores and pays you somewhere around $2 American for each copy sold, you're a writer.

And if you self-publish a 100,000-word novel about vampire soldiers in the Napoleonic era, one which pays you a fraction of a cent for each page that is read, then you're also a writer.

I should know. I've done all of these things, and more besides. Some of them turned out better than others, but they were all satisfying in their own way.

Getting paid to live and write in these strange little worlds, and so many others, has been my dream, my passion, and also my frustration for five years now — and I want to show you how it can be done, so that you can make that journey too…but do it *your* way.

Being a successful writer, entirely on your own terms. That's the dream, right?

Together, we're going to figure out how we can turn your dream into a reality.

My purpose in writing this book is a simple one: to share with you, the soon-to-be-writer, the most important, hard-won lessons that I have learned while building my own writing life. The book is liberally sprinkled with anecdotes taken from my writing journey, all of which explain some of the crucial decisions that I made along that road, and how they impacted my career in ways both good and bad. In this way, you'll be forewarned and better able to avoid the traps and pitfalls I fell into (usually through my own ignorance) and find yourself set up for publishing success.

What You Can Expect

Why do you want to write?

It seems like such a simple question. After all, who *wouldn't* want to be a writer? You're not out there digging ditches in the hot sun, grinding out forty hours a week in an office cubicle devoid of all soul, doing something that feels utterly meaningless; or any one of a thousand other conventional jobs that pay somewhere between 'bare subsistence,' 'okay,' and 'pretty good.'

As a writer, by contrast, you'll whip out your laptop, merrily bang out a few hundred words in the morning (maybe even a thousand or more, if you're feeling particularly motivated) before calling it a day and spending the rest of your time doing whatever you please, while you sit back and just watch those royalty checks roll in.

Oh, if only it were that easy.

Before we embark on our writing journey, it's a good idea to set some realistic expectations. You know those 'get fit, lean, and ripped in only 12 weeks' programs that physical fitness gurus and magazines like to sell? As you more than likely know, they don't really work. Almost everybody that signs up for a get in shape/lose weight fast/get rich quick scheme knows, deep down in their gut, that they're clutching at straws. Speaking as a guy whose waistline is bigger than it ought to be, take it from me: nobody gets fat overnight, and nobody gets rid of their fat overnight, either.

The same is true of writing and publishing.

Your first book, whether it takes you three weeks to write, three months, or even three *years*, almost certainly isn't going to be an overnight success. It doesn't matter whether you publish it yourself, or somehow manage to beat the odds and successfully place it in the hands of a traditional publisher. The story is usually the same: there are virtually no overnight successes in the publishing world any more.

J.K. Rowling's manuscript for *Harry Potter and the Philosopher's/Sorcerer's* (depending upon which side of the Atlantic you are) *Stone* was rejected no less than *twelve times* before a publishing house finally saw the light and put it into print.

Ditto for Frank Herbert's masterpiece *Dune* (twenty times) and Stephen King's *Carrie* (*thirty times!*) These great books, which I chose purely because they are personal favorites of mine, each generated sales that numbered in the millions of dollars, spawning movie adaptations and spinoffs that raked in millions more at the box office. Yet in all three instances, agents and publishers turned them down, not believing that any of them would turn a profit.

Nevertheless, the authors all had one thing in common. All of them believed in their work, persevered, and refused to quit…and the rest, as they say, is history.

When your book finally *does* see print, it's important to understand from the outset that you're not going to make a significant amount of money from it. As a wiser writer than I am once pointed out, it only takes one published book in order to make an author rich — it just so happens that it's usually book number twelve or thirteen.

My first completed book was sold to a traditional publisher

(we'll talk more about that process later) and I was utterly over the moon when I first received an acceptance email for it. It's no exaggeration to say that I was literally shaking with joy. It wasn't long past my fortieth birthday, and I was finally about to crack a lifelong ambition: to see my own name in print.

Writers are imaginative folks by nature, which tends to be a double-edged sword some times. My fertile imagination didn't take long to run away with me. I was going to be a *published writer*, I kept reminding myself, only half believing it. My mind kept conjuring up images of huge royalty checks, signing events at which hordes of eager readers would line up around the block just to pick up my latest book, and perhaps most tellingly of all, a life of luxury in which I would work only when I felt like it, and get to be my own boss.

Idiot.

Hang in there, boy, I remember telling myself more than once, *and before you know it, you'll never have to punch a time clock again!*

Then my first check arrived.

I was getting ready to leave work for the day after what felt like a long shift (I make my living as a paramedic) when my phone pinged. It was a text from my wife.

Looks like you got a check in the mail. The envelope has a publisher's stamp on it.

Looking back, I think I may have actually punched the air in excitement. With an extra spring in my step, I headed to my car and settled in for one of the longest drives home I can ever remember. When I walked through my front door, I found the envelope sitting on the kitchen island, all on its own. My wife had thoughtfully separated it from the rest of the day's mail. She knew that this was going to be a very special moment for me, the culmination of many hours of hard work. That's why she didn't open it herself.

Reaching out, I picked it up with hands that trembled ever so slightly. There it was, the name and return address of the publishing house that had signed me on as an author, clearly stamped on one of the corners. Through the clear plastic window, I could see from the style of paper that this was exactly what she thought it was: a check.

The first money I had ever earned in exchange for words that I had written.

Determined to savor every moment, hoping to burn the experience indelibly into my memory for all time, I slit the envelope open with the greatest of care and pulled out the check. I wanted to appreciate each and every detail of that tiny slip of paper. It was for $500.

The second check for that book, mailed when the manuscript was formally accepted, was for the same amount. $1,000 would be the sum total of my earnings for that first year of writing. Believe me when I tell you that many writers make only a fraction of that in their first year. Was I disappointed? Oh, *hell* yes…but if I had known then what I know now, I would have counted myself lucky to be have even made four figures.

Now, there's obviously no way anybody can live on a grand a year. In fact, once Uncle Sam took his chunk in the form of tax, I'd be left with closer to $700. Nothing to sneeze at, but hardly a living wage. To put it in some kind of perspective, those first two advance checks combined didn't equal two weeks' pay from my regular job.

Just like that, my pie in the sky visions of making a living from having written *In Search of the Paranormal* just evaporated. To tell you the truth, I fell into a bit of a funk. I sat down and did the math. Even if I wrote two or three books a year, assuming that all of them made roughly the same amount of money, all that I'd be left with after taxes was the equivalent of a single mortgage payment to show for it.

Apparently, I wasn't going to be hanging up my stethoscope any time soon.

As things turned out, though, that was a very fortuitous thing for me (although it took me a while to figure that out). I love practicing and teaching emergency medicine, and my writing life now sits very happily alongside my medical career. Together, they form an immensely fulfilling chunk of my overall professional existence. I would come to learn that success in writing isn't a zero sum, all or nothing sort of game. It wasn't a case of "if I'm not making a living doing this, I'm a failure" at all. While I was never going to be a multi-millionaire, neither was I doomed to be a penniless, starving artist, who never made a dime for the words he wrote.

As is so often the case with many things in life, the answer — the sweet spot, if you will — fell somewhere in the middle. At the time of writing, some four years (and fourteen books) after that first book was published, I am now earning between $1,750 and $2,000 per month. To put that into some kind of real-world perspective, my writing is now making my mortgage payments for me. The words that I write are buying me my home, one published book at a time.

That number is also growing with each passing year. In four years, I have increased my writing income more than tenfold. How many other careers can you think of that offer that kind of financial growth, especially in the current godawful economic climate?

Please don't mistake this for bragging. It isn't. The point I'm trying to make is that if I can do this, then so can you. All it takes is a commitment on your part to put in regular, consistent work, and a stubborn refusal to quit.

At the end of the day, it comes down to a simple equation. In publishing, *consistent work + time = success*. I'll show you exactly how I did it, show you how you can do it yourself, and applaud you as you venture forth on your own writing journey.

Trust me, you've got this.

Who is this Guy?

So, just who the heck am *I* to give you any kind of advice on writing and publishing?

Like so many people, I had always wanted to write a book and get it published. I'd dabbled here and there, making more false starts than I could count.

The pattern was always the same. I would put down a few hundred, or in some cases a few thousand words, and then just run out of steam. I'd drift away, distracted, demotivated, or simply bored.

Nothing ever got finished.

All that changed in 2014, when I finally got up the courage to submit a book proposal to a publisher.

It was rejected.

That could so easily have been the end of it, but the rejection letter itself contained one tiny sliver of hope, a doorway to possible publication that had been left cracked open ever so slightly. So, I jumped through it.

After much back and forth, the specifics of which we'll talk about later, that first book finally saw the light of day in 2015. It did relatively well (the first print run completely sold out) and continues to sell decently to this day.
I used that as a springboard to get future books placed with the same publisher, and also with a number of others, with varying degrees of success.

As my back catalog (the term used to describe the number of books an author has written) continued to grow, I became enamored with the process of self-publishing, or as it's commonly called, *indie publishing*. That's not to say that I fell out with my traditional (trad) publishers; I am grateful for every opportunity they have given me to put my words in front of a readership. But the more I looked at the indie realm, the more the grass seemed greener on the other side of the fence.

Rather than switch over to indie entirely, however, I became what is known in writing circles as a *hybrid* author: somebody who self-publishes their own books and also works with trad publishers. To my mind, it really is having the best of both worlds, and I'll be talking about the pros and cons of being a hybrid author as this book progresses. We'll figure out if it's the right path for you, or whether one option or the other would actually be a better fit.

I saw minimal success at first. There were some months when I barely made enough money to go out for dinner once or twice – on my own. But as I released more books, things slowly began to gain traction. Sure, I made a lot of mistakes along the way, but I was learning at every step, diversifying my output and branching out into new forms of media. One was a foray into the realm of audio books, which added an extra stream of income for me at no cost whatsoever.

Things really took a turn for the surreal when suddenly, the TV companies began calling. One producer was putting together a show called *Haunted Hospitals*, which would go on to air on the Travel Channel in the U.S. and numerous other places around the world. They had obviously punched that phrase into Google, because the search engine had promptly come up with my third book, *The World's Most Haunted Hospitals*. Before I knew it, they were flying me to Toronto in order to shoot the show. I would be acting in the capacity as an on-camera 'subject matter expert' in the realm of all things paranormal, giving commentary on people's ghostly encounters.

That, in turn, led to other TV work, which I'm still happily engaged in at the time of writing.

All of it, this great big adventure, snowballed down from that very first book proposal.

I'm rarely the smartest guy in any particular room (unless I happen to be alone) and I don't claim to have been born with any kind of innate talent for writing. What I *am*, however, is a bloody hard worker; one who sits down at the keyboard each and every day, whether I feel like doing so or not, in order to write about the things that fascinate me. This is something that I would willingly do for free, so the fact that people are willing to pay me for the privilege is really just icing on the cake.

We're going to spend the rest of the book talking about how you can do the same thing. Before we get into the specifics, however, there's just one more thing we need to talk about; the one thing that your entire writing career will both stem from and be guided by.

We need to figure out exactly how best to define the nature of success, as it applies specifically to you.

It's easy to be flippant and nonchalantly toss out something like: "I want to make a million dollars." That's actually do-able, believe it or not (over a long enough time frame) but the amount of work that would be required is daunting, to say the least.

How many hours are you willing to spend sitting at a keyboard, away from your family, friends, and the leisure pursuits you love, working toward that million-dollar goal?

Five hours a week?

Ten hours?

Forty?

After spending far too long allowing myself to feel disheartened by the small returns I was getting, especially when I compared them to the number of hours I was putting in, I finally had an epiphany.

Success in writing is whatever *I* say it is, and nothing

else. It's not some arbitrary number, or annual level of income, whether that's $1,000 a year, $10,000 a year, or even $100,000 a year (although that last figure would make me feel pretty successful). True writing success, for me, is all about the journey itself.

I've put thousands of hours into writing by now, with tens of thousands more to go, all being well. I realized that I'd damn well better learn to love the *process* of writing, no matter how much (or little) I was getting paid to do it. Otherwise, I was setting myself up for failure, because I was trading a huge chunk of my life away to do something that wasn't initially all that rewarding, in monetary terms, at least.

Fortunately, I *do* love the writing process. Hopefully you do too — or will, at least once you get up and running. Otherwise, the whole thing will be too much pain for far too little gain. There are many faster and easier ways to make money than sitting at a keyboard and trying to turn your words into something publishable.

For those who stick with it over the long haul, it's a very different story. Because it's such a subjective, deeply personal concept, you're the only one who can define what qualifies as being successful. Maybe you just want to get one book out there, so that you can someday have the satisfaction of walking into your local bookstore and see it sitting there on the shelf. There's absolutely nothing wrong with that; it's the kind of milestone that the vast majority of people never achieve in their lifetime, and one that you should be justifiably proud of.

At the other end of the spectrum, maybe you want to make writing a career. Note that this doesn't have to mean quitting your day job, necessarily, especially if that day job involves doing something you really like. There are plenty of writers who treat their books as a secondary source of income. As the years pass by and their back catalog swells, that can add up to quite a chunk of change.

Or maybe you really do want to shoot for the moon, and aim to make writing your living. That's possible too, with enough time, effort, and raw skull sweat. It won't be easy, and it certainly won't happen overnight, but it *is* do-able.

These are all viable options for you when it comes down to building your best possible writing life.

Before you go any further in this book, please set it aside for a moment and take some time out for a little introspection.

When it gets right down to brass tacks, what is your

ultimate goal? One and done, a series of stories/books, or a lengthy career with your back catalog being measured in double (or even triple) digits?

Once you've answered that question to the very best of your ability — and don't worry about it *too* much, because you can always change your mind later on — we'll move on to the first stage of our journey: deciding what to write.

CHAPTER ONE

Deciding What to Write

For years, aspiring writers have been given the same piece of advice: *Write what you know.*

On the face of it, that's not a bad rule of thumb to follow. It stands to reason that if you're going to write about something (whether it's an article, a blog post, a book, or even an entire series of books) then you'd better have some expertise on that particular subject, especially if you're writing non-fiction. Otherwise, you're just expressing an opinion, and generally speaking, people expect a little more than that when they're being asked to hand over their hard-earned cash in exchange for something you've written.

With that being said, I'd like to propose an amendment to the saying, and it goes like this:

Write what you are passionate about.

If you're a huge fan of science fiction, for example, and are setting out to write your own SF story, it's reasonable to assume that you already know a great deal about the conventions of that particular genre. Although nobody can know exactly what it's like to live on an alien planet, there's no shortage of good SF writers who have transported readers to utterly compelling fictional worlds by way of their stories; places that loom vividly in the imaginations of those who read about them, living on in their memories long after the final page has been turned.

A great case in point involves Frank Herbert, author of *Dune*. The origins of *Dune* lay in a piece of non-fiction writing called *They Stopped the Moving Sands*. Herbert, fascinated by the subject of ecology and the manner in which sand dunes move, found himself sufficiently inspired to do some in-depth research. He then sat down and wrote about it. The subsequent article was never published during his lifetime, but it spawned something much bigger: the book that many readers today believe to be the quintessential science fiction novel.

(Readers who are interested in the full story behind it all can find it in Brian Herbert's superb book *The Road to Dune*).

Over the course of several decades, the world of *Dune* gradually expanded into a rich, fully-realized fictional universe. The novel generated numerous sequels and prequels, a movie directed by auteur David Lynch, a lavish TV mini-series adaptation, and at the time of writing, two big-budget Hollywood movies, the first of which is coming to the silver screen in 2020.

Of course, Frank Herbert had never set foot on an alien world in his life. That just wasn't possible. Thanks to his extensive research, his background in the physical sciences, and above all else, his sheer, unadulterated *passion* for his subject, he was able to conjure up a barren desert planet and a host of diverse, fantastical cultures and political systems with which to populate it, all pulled from his imagination. *Dune* is, in many ways, a completely timeless book. Whenever lists of the so-called 'greatest SF books' are compiled, it always ranks highly, despite having been written more than half a century ago.

Frank Herbert's passion is evident on every page. Whether writing about the cunning machinations of the Bene Gesserit Sisterhood, the centuries-long feud between House Atreides and House Harkonnen, or the mysteries of spice-fueled interstellar travel as navigated by the Spacing Guild, Herbert manages to make it all seem completely authentic and believable.

It's impossible to fake that level of passion for your subject. Nor should you even try.

What is it that *you* are most passionate about? What

inspires you so much that you would sit down for hours upon end and write about it, whether you were getting paid to or not?

For some people, it's cars. For others, it's space opera. Then there's history, both ancient and modern. Romance. Serial killers. Cats. Dogs. Love. Sex. Anger. Hate. Faith. Sports. Dragons. Spies. Submarines. The Wild West.

The list is endless, and it's different for each and every one of us. Maybe baseball is the thing that you love above all else, something that you spend countless hours watching, and you really want to share that passion with readers by writing about the history of the game, and some of its larger-than-life personalities. Or perhaps you have a love of Ancient Greece, and want to write historical fiction, describing the clash of phalanxes in visceral, blood-drenched detail.

For me, that thing is something else entirely.

I'm all about ghosts.

I grew up in a haunted house, for part of my childhood, at least. My grandparents' home in a city called Kingston-Upon Hull, which lies in the north of England, is the source of many happy memories for me. It is also where my obsession with ghosts and what we now like to call 'the paranormal' began.

It's an unremarkable little place, big enough to house a single family, but small enough to realistically be called cozy. My stepfather came from a big family. One of the benefits of that was that I have quite a few aunts and uncles, all of whom are extremely cool people. When they were children, they used to sleep together in shared beds, as was very common back then.

My stepfather used to tell me stories of a kindly old lady, who would come into their communal bedroom at night and tuck the children into bed. None of the kids seemed to think this the least bit odd, and it was only later on that the family came to realize that this was the specter of a former resident, one who was said to have died in the house many years before.

Unlike some of the dark and terrifying ghost stories that are so prevalent today, I find this to be a heartwarming tale. What's not to like about the idea of a sweet old lady keeping a maternal watch over a bunch of innocent young children, years after her death? At least, that's what I think now, at the ripe old age of forty-six. Forty years ago, the very idea of it was terrifying to me.

My stepfather took an almost perverse delight in telling me stories about the phantom, usually just a few short moments before bedtime. It was a calculated move, intended to try and scare the crap out of me. Then I'd have to go upstairs, my sense of dread growing with every step of the way, and crawl into bed in that very same room. I was supposed to sleep in there overnight.

Alone.

I vividly remember it seeming to take forever for me to finally fall asleep. Every creaking floorboard and banging water pipe would jolt me back to wakefulness again. My overactive imagination (usually a handy thing for a writer) was doing me no favors back then. It converted those creaks into stealthy, phantom footsteps, creeping ever closer to the bed in which I lay trembling, dreading a visit from the dead woman I had heard so much about.

Along with the fear, however, came a delicious little thrill, and it's one that has never left me; in fact, it's every bit as strong now as it was back then, if not more so. It's fair to say that ghosts got into my blood when I stayed in that little haunted house, and my fascination for all things ghostly has remained with me throughout my entire life. The old woman

— who never made her presence known to me, despite all of my hopes and fears — lit a spark of passion that still fuels my writing career today. I spent the rest of my childhood (and all of my adulthood) reading everything I could find on the subject of ghosts, the paranormal, and the so-called 'supernatural.'

On the shelves of my local library, I discovered books by paranormal investigators and ghost hunters such as Andrew Green, Peter Underwood, Harry Price, and Guy Lion Playfair, to name just a handful. These men were legends. Their words inspired me. I wanted to be just like them, poking around the dark hallways of historic places, searching for evidence that ghosts really did exist.

Fast-forward four decades, and now I'm fortunate enough to be doing exactly that…and writing about it.

Ghosts are my thing. What's yours? What excites you and inspires you so much that you just *have* to share it with others?

Take some time to reflect and figure out exactly what that thing is. It might be a genre, such as SF, fantasy, romance, or thriller; it could just as easily be a factual subject, like the American Civil War, astronomy, or baking. Whatever it is, you're going to be spending hours of your time exploring it on the page, so it had better be something that moves and fulfills you…a story that you, and *only* you, are uniquely qualified to write.

What will it be?

CHAPTER TWO

Genre, and the Art of Writing to Market

Above everything else, a writer wants one thing: *to be read.*

It's a sad truth that you could write the greatest book imaginable, something truly innovative and unique, put it out into the world, and wait with bated breath…for the damn thing to sell just three or four copies.

All of that effort, pouring your heart and soul into a project, crafting the best book of which you are capable, only to see it disappear into the mists of obscurity. It's extremely disheartening, to say the least.

This happened to me with my first published novel.

For many years, I have been fascinated by the Napoleonic era, particularly the strategy and tactics of warfare during that period. I find some of the larger than life personalities intriguing, particularly men such as Sir Arthur Wellesley, the Duke of Wellington. I once spent a very happy afternoon wandering around Apsley House, the Duke's former residence, situated at the corner of Hyde Park in London. I was enthralled by the personal artifacts that were on display, including uniforms that Wellington had once worn, his personal shaving kit, and even his death mask — a cast that had been taken of the Iron Duke's face shortly after he had died.

Standing there in Wellington's dining room, looking around at the silverware he had used to toast his soldiers after the Battle of Waterloo, I knew that I really wanted to write about the man. Later that same afternoon, I went to Westminster Abbey, walked downstairs into the crypt in which Wellington is buried (alongside another legendary figure of British military history, Admiral Horatio Nelson), and placed a hand on the cold marble surface of the Duke's grave.

At the risk of sounding crazy, I felt a connection. Yes, there was a story to be told about the man. I was sure of it.

The more I thought about it, the more I realized that I wanted to put a fresh spin on the subject. Plenty of books have been written about Wellington, some of them fictional, others biographical in nature. Why re-tread old ground? What hadn't been done before?

After mulling it over for a while and kicking around a few ideas, I finally came to the conclusion that I wanted to do something with a supernatural slant to it. The aristocracy of the late 18th and early 19th centuries had always reminded me of vampires, haughty and aloof, looking down on those they perceived to be inferior. What if, I thought to myself, the Duke and his officer class turned out to be exactly that — vampires?

Armies of living soldiers, led by generals, colonels, and majors who rose from the grave at night to drink the blood of their enemies? *That* hadn't been done before.

Of course, every hero needs a villain. If you're going to introduce vampires, can werewolves (or shape-shifters of some sort) be very far behind? Setting my story in India would be an opportunity to have an antagonist that was a were-*tiger*, part human, part great cat. What about zombies, banshees, and other mythical monsters?

The ideas soon flowed thick and fast. I began plotting out a novel based upon Sir Arthur's campaign against the Sultan of Mysore, who had used his own private army to oppose British rule. Thanks to Wellesley, it hadn't gone well for him, to say the least.

Eighty thousand words later, I had the first draft of a book titled *The Beast of Mysore*. It was to be the first entry in what I was calling the *Wellington Undead* series, one that I envisioned running for several novels and, I hoped, a few short stories. As a fictional universe, I thought that it had great potential — forgetting that, as the author, I was inherently biased.

After edits, two more drafts, and the commissioning of a kick-ass cover, I finally released the book into the world with Amazon's Kindle Digital Publishing as my publisher.

Then I sat back to watch the royalties roll in.

It turned out to be a long wait.

A *very* long wait.

In fact, I'm still waiting.

As I write these words, *The Beast of Mysore* has been out for a little over four years. It has sold just a few hundred copies in all that time, barely making back the money I spent on the cover and finally limping into profitability. Its two sequels, *Goddess of the Dead* and *The Company of Shadows* have been even less successful, sales-wise.

These poor sales came despite a glowing review from bestselling author Doug Dandridge, author of the popular *Exodus: Empires at War* series of SF novels, who loved the book and promoted it to his own readership.

So, I had to ask myself the difficult question: just why did this series tank?

As writers, we owe it to ourselves to be completely honest, so my first thought was: maybe the books just suck. There are certainly better novels out there, by far. Yet, the reviews that the Wellington books have garnered are almost all very positive. Those who read them seem to enjoy them a great deal, and I still receive emails on a regular basis asking me when the next book in the series will be out. (The answer remains: I *will* finish the story off, one day…)

The biggest problem was that I didn't do my research in advance. Not the historical research; I referred to scores of books, establishing the proper techniques, strategies, and minutiae of Wellington's historical period. What I failed to do was to figure out whether there was a potential audience for a series like that, and if so, just how big was it?

When you're writing fiction, knowing your genre is critical. *Genre* is just another way of saying that certain types of books come with very specific reader expectations.

For those who like to read romance novels, there had better be two people falling in love, only to have something (or several somethings) come between them, jeopardizing their chances of ever being together. The more insurmountable the obstacles seem, the more engrossing the story, generally speaking. Think about *Romeo and Juliet*, the timeless tale of star-crossed lovers, whose feuding families contrive to keep them apart…with tragic consequences.

The commonly-accepted trappings of romance novels are things such as love triangles, bitter rivalries, jealousy, unrequited longing, and finally, at the end of the tale, the protagonists come together and live happily ever after…or not, if your name happens to be William Shakespeare. (You can get away with pretty much anything if you're Shakespeare).

If you write a romance novel about a love triangle between a man, a woman, and a sports car that he happens to be obsessed with, you had better find a way for the two lovers to come together in the final act of the book and either ditch the car, or come to some kind of mutual understanding by which they can all coexist peacefully. All stories are ultimately about conflict, which has to be worked through and resolved in order to provide a satisfying experience for the reader.

Let's say that at the end of the story, our hypothetical male protagonist ditches his girlfriend because he realizes that his car is more important to him than any woman could ever be. Your target reader, who expected a certain kind of experience when he or she handed over their money to read a romantic story, is probably going to throw it across the room in disgust. They'll feel cheated (rightfully so) and will be unlikely to ever read anything else you put out ever again.

Genre is, at the end of the day, all about understanding the needs of your readers. All genres have certain specific rules and conventions. As writers, we ignore them at our peril...and that's exactly what I did when I decided to write a book about vampires and were-tigers in 18th-century India. With added zombies.

Looking back on it now, with the benefit of 20/20 hindsight, I've come to see that I gave zero thought to genre when I started the writing process. Just who, exactly, was going to be my audience? Military history buffs, the same readers who devour books by Bernard Cornwell and Steven Pressfield (both excellent novelists) would most likely be put off by the fantastical elements of the tale. The *Wellington Undead* books aren't pure history, and any attempt to pass them off as such would have been nothing short of fraud on my part.

The same holds true with fantasy readers. Although some writers have successfully blended the fantasy genre with the Napoleonic era (Naomi Novak and Susanna Clarke both spring to mind) they represent a very small subset of the fantasy field as a whole. Countless fantasy books chronicle the adventures of dragons, elves, dwarves, and unicorns.

That's not to say that vampires leading armies of British Redcoats don't have their place, but it's not necessarily a niche that is going to attract many fantasy readers, especially those who are looking for something more akin to *The Lord of the Rings*, *Game of Thrones,* or *Warhammer.*

Market Research

Failing to carry out some kind of market research is one of the fundamental pitfalls that you must avoid if you want your book to be successful. Fortunately, it's quite easy to do.

Although there are many places in which your book can be sold, Amazon remains the 800-lb gorilla when it comes to book sales. This is true of both digital and print books. A writer can make a very healthy living from Amazon sales alone, if they go about it in the right way.

My first true bestseller was *Haunted Healthcare*, a collection of non-fiction ghost stories told by nurses, paramedics, and medical patients. One year after its publication, the book continues to regularly top the Amazon bestseller charts in a number of categories.

Amazon follows the extremely handy practice of listing the chart position of each and every book that it sells. At this exact moment in time, *Haunted Healthcare* currently holds the overall sales position of #25,519 in the Kindle chart, which means that 25,518 other books are outselling it. If that sounds bad, be aware that it, in turn, is outselling *millions* of other titles. Including all of the *Wellington Undead* novels.

But that overall sales figure doesn't quite tell you the whole story. Amazon loves to break down its master categories into subcategories, and it's because of this that your book can gain *discoverability* — which means that it will be much easier for the specific readership at whom the book is targeted to discover it.

Haunted Healthcare is currently positioned at #1 in the *Ghosts and Hauntings* subcategory; at #12 in *Supernaturalism*; and at #7 in *Occult Near Death Experiences*.

It's almost impossible for a mere mortal such as you or I to reach the top of the overall Amazon book sales chart; by contrast, it's a *very* achievable goal for you to reach number one in a specific subcategory.

When I first set out to write a non-fiction book about ghosts, the first thing I did was look at similar books, and see which sub-categories they fell into. The fact that these three subcategories even existed told me that there was a solid potential readership for such a book.

We'll explore the concept of Amazon subcategories in greater detail later on, during our discussion of marketing and branding. For now, suffice it to say that your initial market research should involve finding similar books to the one that you intend to write and making a note of their specific subcategories.

Let's say, for the sake of argument, that you're fascinated by the American Civil War, perhaps because one of your ancestors fought in it. Furthermore, after doing some research on him, you've found out the name of his regiment, and would love to write a book about your great-great grandfather and his fellow soldiers as they marched and fought their way through the war.

A small amount of poking around on Amazon shows the following subcategories: *U.S. Civil War Regimental Histories* and *History of American Civil War Regiments*. They sound exactly the same, don't they?

Clicking on the first category shows us what the top ten bestselling books are for that category. In prime position is a regimental history of the 6th Wisconsin Volunteers, a very specific subject indeed. The second and third books are more generalized, being the classic *Lee's Lieutenants* and *Mr.*

Lincoln's Army. Then we find *A Broken Regiment: The 16th Connecticut's Civil War*, another book that sounds very much like the one you plan to write.

Next comes *A History of the Ninth Regiment: Illinois Volunteer Infantry, With the Regimental Roster*.

Keep on clicking your way down, and you'll see the entire top one hundred books in each of those Civil War subcategories. Sure enough, there *is* a target audience for books about specific Civil War regiments. You can now rest assured that when you finish your book and release it, there'll be a readership that you have a good chance of selling it to.

Now that you've figured out what it is that you're going to write about, spend a little time searching the subcategories on Amazon until you find one that fits that topic as closely as possible. Look at the top ten, to get an idea of which specific type of book is selling best; then scan the rest of the top one hundred, to get a general feel for the rest of that sub-genre. These books are all selling, albeit some better than others.

This is your potential market, the one you're going to write to in order to be successful. It's worth comparing and contrasting the different titles and reading a few reviews, both good and bad; it puts your finger on the pulse of the readership, telling you what worked for them about each book and what didn't.

A Winning Formula

Despite the obvious benefits of writing to a given market, if that's your only rule, the chances are that you're in for a miserable time. Let's say you realize that there's a great market for technological thrillers, jam-packed full of car chases, explosions, and gunfights. There are big bucks to be made in that particular genre, as writers such as Lee Child or Mark Greaney can readily attest. Those guys regularly top the *Conspiracy Thrillers* and *Military Thrillers* subcategories, raking in a small fortune in the process. Wouldn't it be nice to cut yourself a slice of that pie?

There's just one catch. What you really want to write is the mathematicians who broke the German Enigma codes during World War II.

There's certainly a market for the former, it's true; but if your heart lies elsewhere, attempting to put out 100,000 words of the next Jason Bourne clone isn't going to make you happy. If it becomes too much of a drag, you most likely won't even finish it, and even if you do, the lack of passion in your writing will show through. You'll feel like a hack, and the process of writing will soon become more of a chore than a pleasure. It quickly turns into a job, rather than a joy, with all of the stress and frustration that a job entails…and who needs more of *that* in their life?

You have a much greater chance of making a splash in the *World War II Espionage* or *Political Intelligence* categories with your code-breaking labor of love than you would in the techno-thriller arena, which is almost exclusively dominated by the juggernauts, those writers whose books always line the shelves whenever you're browsing for something to read at the airport.

What it basically boils down to is this:

Writing just to the market alone can crush your soul.

Writing only in accordance with your passions and interests won't necessarily sell well.

The answer is to find the sweet spot where the two coincide, rather like a Venn diagram.

Your passion subject + writing to market = SUCCESS.

That's it. It really is no more complicated than that. In an ever-expanding book market, it's almost guaranteed that there's a niche for you. The trick is figuring out exactly where that niche is, and making it work for you. I recommend browsing the multitude of Amazon sub-categories before you settle upon your final subject of choice, and make sure that there's some level of readership for your chosen topic.

Once that's done, it's time to answer the next critical question: just how do you get the bloody thing *written?*

CHAPTER THREE

Getting it Written

Before we get down to the nuts and bolts of the actual planning and writing process, I want to start out with a word or two about research. Some authors absolutely *love* doing research for their book projects; for others, it's about as enjoyable as getting a root canal.

I tend to fall somewhere in the middle. For my non-fiction books, I spend a lot of time actually *living* the adventure I'm writing about. Several times each year, I get to pack my bags and head out to investigate some allegedly haunted location for a few days, usually moving in and spending a few nights there, doing weird things with weird people.

While I'm there, I interview witnesses, delve into historical records, look at architectural plans, and gather as much data as I can about the case I'm working on. That's my research. Sometimes it's relatively simple and straightforward; on other occasions, it can be convoluted and a bit of a pain, but it's never less than interesting.

Research also means hitting the books. For the *Wellington Undead* series, I referred constantly to a stack of some 30+

books in order to get the minutiae of life in 18th century India down. I wanted to make my portrayal of the time and setting as accurate as possible (vampires and werewolves notwithstanding).

Unfortunately, carrying out research can sometimes work against you. It's a bit of a rabbit hole, one that it's far too easy to go down and get lost. Yes, knowing exactly how a Brown Bess musket was readied, loaded and fired is useful information to have when writing a book like *The Beast of Mysore*, but more importantly, every hour spent researching is an hour spent NOT WRITING. If you're a procrastinator, as many of us are to some degree, then "I was doing my research" can easily become one of the most convenient excuses imaginable for not actually working on your manuscript. Most writers I know have fallen in to this trap at one time or another, losing entire *days'* worth of productivity because they were hitting the books, surfing the web, or (horror of horrors) sucked into a Youtube death spiral from which there is no escape.

A great recommendation from author Steven Pressfield is to limit yourself to just three sources of research at the very most when you first start writing. Three books, three websites, three documentary shows. No more than that.

Why? Because it removes that excuse for not writing, and paradoxically, a lot of writers — myself included — find that when they're about to embark on a project, the idea of not writing suddenly becomes very attractive. It's a psychological phenomenon that I've fallen prey to over and over again. I love the period of time before I start work on a book, when it is nothing more than a shining mass of potential. Not a single word has been written yet. It's all just a dream in my head, an unsullied concept. I also love it when the book finally comes out, and I can hold a physical copy of it in my hands. There's no feeling quite like it in the world. But as for the bit in the middle…

…well, that's an ugly, messy process at the best of times, even when it's going relatively well. There's a voice in the back of almost every writer's mind, a silky-smooth, vicious little bastard that likes nothing more than to slink out from whatever dark rock it lurks behind to come out and play mind games with you, just for its own amusement.

Its name, thanks once again to Steven Pressfield, is *Resistance*, and we'll come back to that irritating little turd in a while. For now, though, just understand that one of the primary symptoms of Resistance is an inability to get your project started. Researching their chosen topic *ad infinitum* is one way in which writers stumble right at the starting gate, no matter how experienced they may be.

Don't be one of them.

Let's say you're writing a historical novel about ancient Rome. You have a fairly decent idea of the setting, the story, how it's all going to turn out in the end, and who the main characters are. But you're kicking off with a battle scene, and you realize there's a lot about the Roman art of warfare you don't know. Time to crack open the books!

Two days later, you still haven't written a word — because you want to get those details nailed down to the point of perfection. What type of sandal did a Roman Legionary wear? How high was it, and how was one laced up? What about the helmet of a Centurion – what color was the horse-hair crest, and did it run from back to front or side to side? What color should his tunic be? His armor? His sword—

And so on, and so on…to the point of data overload.

The way to avoid this trap is to go ahead and write your battle scene to the very best of your ability, perhaps referring to a source or two every once in a while. Once the first draft of your book is done, once you've finally crossed the finish line and can state with total confidence that you aren't going to abandon it partway through, you can cycle back and start filling in all the details that you missed. Think of it as being a bit like refining a sketch, fleshing out the light and dark areas, adding contrast and color where they're needed.

Although it's poor grammar to say so, the truth is that you can't edit nothing. The worst piece of work that you see through to completion is better than the best thing that never made it to the finish line. I've often wondered how many truly great — or even just halfway decent — books never saw the light of day, purely because the writer bogged down in the details and never saw it through to the end.

Fail.

Research has its place, or more accurately, places. Those places are partially up-front, but primarily after the fact, when the dust has settled on your first draft and you have typed the words THE END.

Don't research your manuscript to death.

Format and Structure

Whether fiction or non-fiction, every book has to have a format and a structure. Sometimes it's the traditional three-act structure that is so beloved of novelists and screenwriters everywhere (and with good reason — it works). It can also be non-traditional; beginning at the end of the story, say, and working backward in time to the precipitating incident.

A lot of the non-fiction books I write are structured in a chronological narrative style, bringing the reader along with me as I venture into a haunted location and uncover what I can there. Readers tell me that they like it because it evokes the sensation of them being a part of my team, discovering things as I discover them and experiencing the same surprises.

Other format examples include the encyclopedia-type book, with various entries grouped together under a common theme. I wrote *The World's Most Haunted Hospitals* along those lines, listing some of…well, the world's most haunted hospitals, and detailing some of the ghostly encounters that are said to have taken place within their walls. The structure of that book is like a series of spokes on a wheel, all extending outward from a central hub, or premise.

The format of the book is the form it's going to take — traditional narrative, entry-based, textbook, etc. The structure is the foundation, the guide-posts that you're going to follow during the writing process that will get you through to the end; a series of beats that act as a road map to your final destination.

Planning vs. Pantsing

There are, broadly speaking, two ways to write your book: *planning* and *pantsing.*

Planners sit down and outline the book before typing a single word of text that the reader will ever get to actually read. Sometimes, a plan or outline can be relatively brief: one highly respected novelist recommends that the outline for a novel should never exceed one side of A4 paper in length. This provides structure, but also keeps a lot of the details abstract, allowing the writer to fill them in as she goes along. For example, a main character may have to die in an ambush halfway through the novel. That's going to be part of your plan. The fact that they're going to be stabbed repeatedly in the chest with another character's Bowie knife which was accidentally dropped and then picked up by their half-crazed father-in-law, is a detail that you may only discover when the time comes to actually write the scene. It'll surprise you as much as it does the reader. That's one of the joys of writing fiction.

Pantsers, on the other hand, get their name from the fact that they like to fly by the seat of their pants. Prolific author Dean Wesley Smith sometimes refers to this method as 'writing into the dark.' It involves literally sitting down in front of a blank screen and just starting to write, often with no more than a general idea of where you're heading, and seeing where the words take you. Take a character or two, throw them into a situation, and see what happens.

Pantsing can be a highly effective way of writing — for the right person. The question is, are you one of those people? I've pantsed a few pieces of fiction in my time, and while they've been tremendous fun to write, the writing process always came along with a worrisome sense of unease. Where was the story going? How was it going to end? Could I even *finish* it? Planning your work out in advance, even at a fairly abstract, thirty-thousand-foot level, brings along with it a certain feeling of security.

The outline for the book you're currently reading ran close to two thousand words. For longer books, it's not unusual for me to go three or four thousand words.

I use a program named Scrivener for my writing. Despite having a fairly steep learning curve, it's popular with a lot of authors. One helpful aspect of the software is that it allows for the creation of a series of discrete sections, which can be used to break your book up into parts, chapters, and even scenes, if you want to get that granular with it.

The high-level outline for this book looks like this:

> *Foreword*
> *Introduction*
> *Deciding what to write*
> *How to write it*
> *Traditional or self-published*
> *Marketing and Branding*
> *Your next project (and your next, and your next…)*
> *Summing up*

That's it. Twenty-eight words. That's an outline. It provides me with a structure, albeit a very generalized one. It is enough to get me started, but I like to incorporate a little more detail into my outlines, so I expand each section in Scrivener and then add in a series of bullet points.

The outline for the upcoming sections looks like this:

Where do I start? (Doesn't have to be the beginning)

Where am I going?
> *Include a sample structure outline of this book*

Good writing habits
- *Setting a daily word count*
  - *Sticking to it no matter what (almost)*
  - *Something is always better than nothing!*
    - *One paragraph. One line. One **sentence**.*

  - *But I can't find the time…*
    - ***Make** the time!*

  - *Jedi mind tricks*
  - *Don't break the chain of Xs*
  - *Getting paid to write (lunch break etc)*
  - *You don't **have** to write, you **get** to write*

Resistance
- *Steven Pressfield (The War of Art)*
- *Resistance is a bastard but you can beat it*
- *Power on through*
- *Get to the finish no matter what*
- *Edit edit edit your own work*
- *Rewrite as needed*
  - *Line editor*

Copy editor

Know when to stick a fork in it and call it done
Good enough is good enough

Proofreading
You will suck at this
Pay somebody to do it

On to the next one

Each line provides me with the bare bones of another subsection of the book. Each one is a 'beat,' and the process of actually writing will be made immeasurably easier because I took the time to outline them before jumping right in. Without these beats, the book would undoubtedly be a lot less coherent. Instead, it has a logical progression, stepping you, the reader, through the process of going from "I want to write a book" all the way to "my book is done and ready for publication."

The sentences that are more closely aligned to the left margin are the major beats, the significant points that I definitely have to hit. The lines beneath them, which move further to the right, are sub-topics that expand upon the main point. When it came to writing the bulk of this book, these master topics and sub-topics were my blueprint, making sure that I stayed on track during the construction of the manuscript.

I'm a firm believer that spending a few hours to plan out your book before you start writing will pay huge dividends in the long run. There are few worse feelings for a writer than getting lost in the middle of a manuscript, usually somewhere in the great nebulous morass known as 'the middle.'

Beginnings are relatively easy. Tying things together at the end isn't usually all that difficult. But everything in between…well, *there's* the rub.

CHAPTER FOUR

Where do I Start?

At the beginning, right? Isn't it obvious?

Well, frankly, no it isn't...

Yes, a story, whether fact or fiction, has a beginning, a middle, and an end...at least, it *should.* That doesn't mean you *have* to start writing on page one, however. Movies aren't shot chronologically; the bigger the production, the more complicated its shooting schedule, and in order to save time and money, scenes will often be filmed out of sequence. It isn't unusual for the most dangerous stuff to be shot last, for fear of one of the stars getting hurt and hampering the shoot.

The same also holds true with books. Sometimes it makes more sense to start writing in the middle of the book, or at the end, and then work your way backwards. When I wrote *The Horrors of Fox Hollow Farm* with my co-writer Robert Graves, I began writing from the mid-point in the book, because that's where I personally entered the story. It was easier for me to kick my section off with things that were personal memories, events that I had actually lived through.

The words soon flowed thick and fast, and once the second half of the book was done, I cycled back to the beginning in order to help document the experiences of Robert, his family, and other witnesses, not to mention the true story of the serial murders that had been committed at the farm. By the time I got to the first part of the book, the pressure was off. The ending was already written to my satisfaction, so I wasn't writing into the dark. That gave me a huge confidence boost.

I'm a paramedic by profession, and all paramedics are trained to carry out triage at mass casualty incidents. This involves determining who has a realistic chance of survival, who most likely doesn't, and how best to prioritize between them. Performing triage is a difficult and daunting prospect, not least because first responders can easily be overwhelmed by the sheer volume of wounded and dying patients that they are being asked to deal with.

Where do you begin? The young child who is screaming because her leg is fractured? The middle-aged man who is shot in the arm, but whose bleeding is controlled by a tourniquet? Or the vomiting old lady with shrapnel embedded in her face?

The answer is a simple one: you start where you stand.

That's the principle we teach during initial EMT and paramedic training. No matter how bad things look when you are surrounded by chaos and carnage and the whole world is coming apart around you, the well-trained first responder goes to the nearest human being and starts triaging right then and there.

Start where you stand.

It's that simple. The same principle applies to your manuscript. When you're ready to start writing (and assuming that you have an outline, you *are* ready to start writing — don't convince yourself otherwise!) just pick a section of the outline that appeals to you. What's that, you say? None of them appeal to you, particularly? Fine. Then close your eyes, jab your finger at the screen, and see which section it lands on.

Start writing there.

CHAPTER FIVE

Where am I Going?

You're not going to get lost, my friend. Unless you're a pantser (in which case, unfortunately, you're pretty much on your own here) then you will always have an outline to light your way. Bear in mind that the only thing that stands between you and completion is a *finite* number of unwritten words. All you have to do is fill in the blanks.

If that sounds flippant, it's not meant to be. Writing is daunting. I totally get that…particularly if you haven't written anything for publication before. But the chances are that you write hundreds, if not thousands of words each week, if you're writing emails, notes, term papers, or anything of a similar nature.

How do you eat an elephant? One bite at a time.

Almost every book is a series of chapters.

Every chapter is a series of pages.

Every page is a series of paragraphs.

Every paragraph is a series of sentences (or sometimes just one).

Every sentence is a series of words.

Your job, in a nutshell, is to generate words, and then turn those words into sentences. Those sentences will quickly become paragraphs, which in turn will become pages, then chapters, and before you know it, you'll have yourself a completed manuscript.

It may not be *good* (that will come later) and it may not be pretty, but neither of those things are important.

What matters is that it gets *finished*.

Everything else is secondary. Once you get started, it's all about pushing through to the end. Nothing else matters

Momentum is your friend, and resistance, that miserable ever-lurking naysayer, is your blood enemy. When you start into a writing sprint, it's often possible to hit a point of critical mass, where the process seems to take on a life of its own.

Before you know it, you're in a flow state that is a weird form of creative nirvana. You find that the words come thick and fast, almost more quickly than your fingers can type (one reason why some writers prefer to use dictation software instead of a keyboard, though I've never been a fan of that particular method).

You're on a roll, and there's not a thing in the whole wide world that can stop you…is there?

Developing Good Writing Habits

At forty-six years of age, I can honestly say that I'm in shape.

Unfortunately for me, that shape is something that bears a definite resemblance to a bag of potatoes.

Like a lot of writers, I tend to spend far too much time with my arse in a chair, pecking away at a keyboard, and far too little in the gym, or out and about enjoying the wonders of nature.

Now don't get me wrong: I'd *love* to have a more muscular build, with bulging biceps, a V-shaped waist, rippling six-pack abs…you know, the sort of physique that makes members of the opposite sex swoon. (Or the same sex. Whatever floats your boat).

I'm totally capable of it, too. I know I am. All it would take is for me to work out consistently and watch what I eat.

Easier said than done, right?

True success, the kind of long-term success that is the only sort really worth having in life, does not materialize overnight. It comes in tiny increments, the product of small, regular changes; the little habits that are built upon one good decision at a time, all of them strung together in a long chain that stretches out over the course of days, weeks, months, and ultimately, years.

You're not going to sit down and write a book overnight, no matter how fast a typist you are. Writing success is all about the long haul, so allow me to introduce you to your new best friend and worst enemy combined: the daily word count.

CHAPTER SIX

Your Daily Word Count

I once read an article by the renowned bodybuilder, action movie star, and politician Arnold Schwarzenegger, in which he talked about his recommended techniques for weight training. I'm paraphrasing here, but the Austrian Oak said that if he was bench-pressing, say, five hundred pounds, and you're pressing one hundred, both of you are working at maximum capacity. It isn't the actual *weight* that matters, he emphasized; it's the fact that both of you are working as hard as you possibly can, using every last ounce of the baseline strength that each of you possesses.

The same is true when it comes to writing. If you set a daily word count and strive to meet it, the actual number itself is less important than the fact that you achieve that goal consistently.

Writing is like exercise; indeed, it *is* a form of exercise, albeit one for the brain rather than for the body. A good way to picture the act of writing on a daily basis is something akin to developing a 'writing muscle.' The more of it you do, the better at it you tend to become.

This is why keeping up a daily word count is so essential. It guarantees you a regular dose of authorial exercise. Small, daily gains add up to huge benefits in a surprisingly short period of time.

The 'average' paperback book (if there is such a thing) generally runs to about 250 words per page. Adult novels tend to run somewhere between 80,000 and 100,000 words. Children's and Young Adult (YA) fiction usually falls between 50,000 and 60,000 words. My own fiction hovers between 70,000 and 100,000 words, and my non-fiction books come in at anywhere between 35,000 words to 60,000. With that being said, I've just finished a non-fiction paranormal collaboration that ended up being 80,000 words, and am currently contracted to write a book about serial killers that will come in somewhere around 150,000. (Just between you and me, I'm not daunted – I'm *terrified*).

Those are some big, scary numbers, but if you break them down, they don't seem nearly as intimidating. I'm willing to bet that you've written emails that are fifty words in length, or possibly even longer. Let's stick with fifty for now, just to keep things simple.

Fifty words per email, multiplied by five emails, in the space of one day. That's 250 words, or, as I like to think of it, one page of printed text.

Multiply that by 100 days, and you have 25,000 words. 200 days, you're at 50,000 words…and that, my friend, is a book. In less than seven months' time.

In fact, it may be more than a book. Times are changing, and what we typically think of as 'a book' — those things we see on the shelves at Barnes and Noble, Waterstones, or whichever is your favorite book store — is now more an example of the old way of thinking than a truly objective standard. When it comes to the realm of digital publishing, a 'book' is any kind of digital document that a reader is willing to pay money for. There are 'books' available for sale out there that are only 1,000 – 5,000 words long (little more than a short story) and plenty that come in at the 10,000, 15,000, or 30,000-word mark.

No longer does something need to have a thick spine in order to be sold as a book. You don't ever want to rip the customer off (I sell my short stories for a dollar or two at most) but at the end of the day, your readers are the ones who will determine what price they are willing to pay in exchange for whatever it is that you've written. As long as it brings value to the reader, in the form of useful knowledge, diversion, or entertainment, then both of you have benefited from the deal, and everybody's happy.

When it comes to the world of digital publishing, there's no minimum page count any more. This is especially true if you self-publish. You don't have to worry about an editor mandating that you write X-thousand words, whether you have something valuable to say or not. Manuscripts don't have to be padded. You can keep them lean and clean.

One thing to bear in mind, however, is that you'll almost certainly want to publish the finished product in print form as well as in the digital format. People are understandably wary of 'books' that appear to be little more than pamphlets, and are usually reluctant to hand over their hard-earned cash for them.

Potential readers who are browsing the digital shelves of Amazon or other online readers are presented with your book's cover, a synopsis, and other material, such as reviews and a star rating from 1-5. Assuming that they find all this to be of interest, and don't simply click on by to the next title, the more experienced shopper will then look at your book's price, and its page count.

A 39-page 'book' for $3.99 — does that seem like good value for money? The chances are that it won't to the average customer. Some readers will balk at paying *anything* for a 39-page book, though your chances of success are greater if you're only asking $0.99 or a similarly modest sum. It's going to be a lot harder for you to turn a profit on something that short, particularly if you have to price it as low as the online retailer will allow you to, in order to make it a somewhat attractive prospect.

Page count matters. As with so much in life, there's a sweet spot, a certain point at which your piece of work becomes an actual *book* in the mind of the potential reader, as opposed to a gimmick or a joke. In terms of the word count, short is fine, but *too* short isn't.

At the end of the day, *you* must be the judge. It's worth noting that if your finished work is less than a hundred printed pages in length, the physical edition will most likely not have room on the spine for the title and author name. In other words, when it sits on a bookshelf, the only thing visible will be the crease in the spine; no words or lettering will show up, because the binding is too thin to print anything on. I have always promised myself never to release a book in print that is so short that the title won't fit on the spine. So far, it's a promise that hasn't been difficult to keep.

Then again, maybe physical print editions aren't something you're overly bothered about. The vast majority of profit for self-published authors these days comes from the digital realm. Only a relatively small percentage comes from print editions. If holding an actual paper copy of your book in your own hands isn't a priority for you, feel free to ignore what I've just said and tailor your e-book to whatever length you'd like and price it as you see fit.

Now, back to the daily word count. 250 words a day gives you one page. Once your book is outlined and you have a decent idea of where you're going with it, you can complete the first draft of a 200-page book in 200 days, or a 100-page book in a little over three months. Suddenly, getting that book written doesn't look like such an insurmountable obstacle, does it?

The trick is to stick with it, through rain or shine, in sickness or in health. My daily word count is set at 1,000 words. That, by the way, is a *minimum*. Often, I'll do more. It's not unusual for me to have 3,000 — 5,000-word days, especially if I get into the zone and the words are really flying. But I make it a rule to never go to bed without having put at least 1,000 words in the bank. I find it hard to turn out the light and go to sleep unless I know that I've hit that magic number.

In my kitchen, mounted on the wall directly facing the

pantry, is a dry erase board. On it are written the names of all of the book projects I am currently working on. At any given time, I usually have four or five titles in various stages of development. All of them are written in black ink. Then there are roughly the same number of ideas/concepts that haven't been fully fleshed out yet, but that I plan on getting around to eventually.

Next to each one, written in bright red erasable ink, is a number: that's the word count. Looking at my board right now, I can see the following:

FORT MIFFLIN — 2,500
SERIAL KILLERS — 6,000
THE HANGING PIT — 13,337
GACY'S GHOST — 13,035
BUILDING THE WRITE LIFE — 9,089
CRIPPLE CREEK —
OSPH —
VILLISCA —
MONROE HOUSE —

The Fort Mifflin book will focus upon a Revolutionary War-era fort located on the Delaware River, not too far away from the city of Philadelphia. Earlier this summer, I spent a week there, investigating both the history and haunting. On the flight back from Philly to Denver, I wrote up a 2,500-word outline in Scrivener, while the events of my stay were all still fresh in my mind. That book is now prepped and waiting to be written, once I finish some of my other ongoing projects.

Serial Killers is a long-term project, with only 6,000 words out of 150,000 in the bank. Half of that is outline, and there'll be more outlining to be done once the project really picks up steam. It's still in its incipient stages at the moment, though. Most of the book is scheduled to be written over the course of the Christmas holidays (it's August as I write this).

The Hanging Pit and *Gacy's Ghost* are both fully outlined and each has 13,000+ words apiece written. I am actively working on *Gacy's Ghost* in tandem with this book, putting in about 5,000 words a week on it. I'll switch over to finish *The Hanging Pit* once that's done.

The four projects at the bottom of the list haven't been started yet, but I already know that they will be my first book projects for 2020. They exist only inside my brain at the moment, with the exception of a few written and audio notes, but I put them on the board as a reminder of where

I'm heading as a writer over the course of the next year.

When I got out of bed this morning, this book stood at 9,089 words, including the outline. Today has been an in-the-zone kind of day, because the clock is just now coming up on midnight and my updated word count is 13,894. I'll close out the day at around 5,000 words (14,000 is a nice round number, don't you think?) go to bed, and sleep like a baby, content with having hit my daily 1,000 and also putting a few thousand extra words in the bank on top of the minimum

Before I crawl into bed, however, I get to practice my nightly ritual. I'll stand in front of the whiteboard, erase the number 9,089 with my thumb, and then replace it with a revised word count: somewhere in the region of 14,000.

Then I can sleep.

I'm telling you this not to brag, but to illustrate the way in which having a daily word count fits into the writing life. It's now as much a part of my daily routine as brushing my teeth, eating breakfast, or walking the dog. These aren't things I have to decide whether I'm going to do or not; they simply *are*, and the fact that they'll get done is a given.

Remember, *writers write,* come hell or high water.

If you're just starting out as a writer, don't try to hold

yourself to 1,000 words per day — at least, not at first. Arnie didn't start out bench pressing 500-lb barbells. Start with 250 words, that magic single page. If you feel like doing more, that's great! Push on. But no matter what happens, once you've hit that daily word count, allow yourself to breathe a small sigh of self-satisfaction and grant yourself the freedom to put your feet up and relax. Remember to spend some time with your family, or enjoy doing the things that you love. Having a life beyond the keyboard is critically important to staying sane, and it's far too easy to forget that when you're hunched over a laptop all the time.

My wife sometimes refers to herself as a 'writing widow,' and she's only halfway joking. Being married to an author can be a pretty thankless situation sometimes. It's far too easy for us to become engrossed in what we're doing, playing around in whichever world we're building and interacting with inside of our own heads. As a consequence, it's all too easy for us to disengage from the material world around us. That way lies danger, if taken to excess.

Once you hit that daily word count, save the file, update your personal whiteboard, notebook, or however it is you plan to track your word count, and then give yourself permission to shut down the laptop or tablet and get back to reality. You've earned it, and so have the people and animals who care about you. What good does it do you to become a successful writer if it costs you the very things that make life worth living?

I often get asked whether I *really* write 1,000 words every single day, no matter *what* is happening in my personal life.

The answer is, of course, a qualified 'no.'

I'm a dog person, and thanks to the influence of my wife, a cat person too. I inherited a menagerie of black cats when we first got married, and the furry little buggers have a way of burrowing their way into your heart, digging their murder mittens in, and not letting go. Ever.

When one of my beloved pets dies, I become nothing short of a physical and emotional wreck. I can't turn out 1,000 words on a day like that, and I'm not going to pretend that I can. I can barely see the bloody screen through the tears.

I'll never forget the night that my beloved dog, Greta, had to be put to sleep at home. I was about as miserable as I've ever been in my entire life. I was overseas in the U.K. at the time, investigating a supposedly haunted prison for witches, when she was suddenly taken ill. My poor wife had to shoulder the entire burden while I was stuck 5,000 miles away, feeling utterly helpless and bereft.

She held Greta close and hugged her while the kindly vet sent her to her eternal rest, then called me to let me know that my sweetheart of a pup had passed peacefully, with her mum whispering in one of Greta's ham-like ears that her daddy loved her more than anything in the world.

After I hung up the phone, I burst into tears. Stuck in a strange English city, all alone at three o'clock in the morning, I began to aimlessly wander the streets. I hadn't the slightest idea of where I was going, and just started to take turn after random turn, following the street lights, but not really seeing them through the haze of tears.

With hindsight, it was a stupid thing to do. I could easily have found myself in a dangerous part of town and gotten mugged. Then again, I pity anybody who had gotten in my way that night with the intent of causing trouble, because with the amount of pent-up rage and despair I felt inside, I could easily have pummeled them into a pulp without thinking twice.

Before long, I found myself standing at the sea front. I was so upset that for one second — just *one* split second — I seriously considered jumping off the cement wall into the ocean and ending it all. I really was *that* upset and irrational.

I stood there for I don't know how long, just listening to the waves crashing upon the shore. Finally, shaking my head, I turned around and went back to my hotel. When I got back to the room, I fired up my tablet and began to write.

Fuck this, I wrote, fingers pounding the keyboard in a seething outburst of unleashed anger. *So unfair. It's so goddamned unfair. I miss her so much. I'm half the world away when she needs me the most. Fuck my life.* FUCK. MY. LIFE.

Then I shut the tablet down and cried myself to sleep.

Total word count for the day: 29.

I wrote a book about my experiences in the witches' prison, titled *Spirits of the Cage*. I didn't mention Greta, or my ramble around the deserted early-morning streets. The following year, however, I wrote another book for the same publisher, and in this one (*Trail of Terror*) I took those twenty-nine words and turned them into a few hundred. Greta's story fit beautifully into one of the chapters of that particular book, and despite the fact that I just had a handful of pained and angry sentences on file from that night, the act of simply re-reading them took me right back to the sea front, and allowed me to write about it from a place of greater peace and clarity.

As things turned out, I *did* hit my word count for that night. It just took me another year to do it.

Even on one of the darkest of nights of my life, I was able to write *something*. Not only that, but that particular 'something' turned out to be extremely useful in a completely unforeseen way. The lesson I took from that experience was that you should always write *something*, no matter how small, humble, or pointless it might seem at the time.

Writing something is *always* better than writing nothing!

If it's all that you can manage, write a paragraph. Just one paragraph.

If you can't manage that, write one *line*, or one *sentence*. A word or two, if that's really all you can do. But write *something*.

Write. Something.

Then update your daily total, go to bed, and sleep like a baby.

Because you're a writer, and that's what writers do.

CHAPTER SEVEN

Jedi Mind Tricks

"I'd love to write a book, but I just can't find the time..."

That's probably the most common thing people say to me whenever we're talking about the business of writing. It seems as though everybody would like to have their name on a book, but life just has a habit of getting in the way sometimes.

I can relate. I work a full-time job as a paramedic clinical chief, with forty hours in the office and anywhere between ten to twenty-four hours more spent working on the streets in the 911 system, teaching classes, and performing various other duties.

In addition to that, I moonlight as an instructor in two different EMT (Emergency Medical Technician) and paramedic academies, chair several medical committees, and also attend a series of regular events in the paranormal field.

It's a lot, and sometimes the last thing I want to do is walk in the door at 10:30 at night, take off my boots, sit down and start writing. I want to kick back in front of the TV, or lose myself in a good book for a while until I finally fall asleep.

But there it is, nagging away at me from the corner of my kitchen: that bloody whiteboard and its daily word count total. At this point in my life, I've conditioned myself to knock out that thousand words before allowing myself to truly relax.

We all have the same twenty-four hours granted to us each day, and the hard truth of it is, we make time for the things that really matter to us. People who place a high value on personal fitness (I really wish I was one of them) will find a way to work out, no matter how tough and draining their day was.

They might take a brisk walk during their lunch hour, or find a way to climb a few flights of stairs over the course of the working day.

I know medics who do push-ups on the hood of their ambulance, or walk in circles around it while they're waiting at post for the next 911 call to come in. They're militant about hitting the 10,000 steps that their Fitbits insist upon as a daily target.

These people have become adept at finding creative ways to crowbar some fitness training into their day, no matter how little free time they have available.

It's therefore possible to approach writing in the same

way. All of my books are written on an iPad Pro, which comes with a magnetized keyboard. All of the files upload to my Dropbox automatically. This allows me to string together a few hundred words, or even just a few paragraphs, whenever I have a little dead time to spare in my day.

Recently, I took a road trip to Chicago. With one of my friends taking a long stretch handling the chore of driving (thank you, Linda), I sat in the passenger seat with my tablet propped on my knees and wrote 3,000 words. On a recent flight to Atlanta, I got in 1,000, and still had time to relax with a Jack Reacher novel before landing. In both cases, I was using otherwise 'dead time' —- time that usually can't be spent on anything productive — to get my word count in.

The chances are that no matter how busy you are, you have a lot of dead time built into your working day, no matter how efficiently you try to plan it out in advance. Maybe you're waiting at the dentist's or doctor's office for your appointment. That's five, perhaps ten minutes in which you could knock out fifty words. Or a hundred. Don't have a tablet or a laptop handy? Get a pocket notebook and write freehand, then transcribe it afterwards. Have a transcription day at the weekend, and type out all of your handwritten writing into a master Word file (or whatever is your word processor of choice).

You're riding the bus to work. Taking your lunch hour, or even just a fifteen-minute break in the middle of your working day. Relaxing on the couch after dinner. The kids have just been put to bed. Each one of these tiny slivers of time is fair game, a brief window of opportunity for putting down a few lines. All it takes is the discipline to do so, a discipline that will be born out of a new habit that you'll slowly but surely form by doing this every single day.

I know people who write in the bath; others who write on the toilet (never, ever ask to borrow their tablet); still others who put down words in the kitchen while waiting for dinner to cook; these people will work on their book in any one of a hundred different times and places during the day. A little creativity and willingness to jot down a few lines is the key thing here. Remember: small gains, consistently made, and you're well on the path to success.

Bottom line: buy a notebook, keep it with you at all times. If you get to bedtime and haven't hit your word count, take it to bed with you and write a little before turning out the light. You'll sleep better, I promise.

If writing is even remotely important to you, you'll make the time for it. That isn't to say that it will be easy; it almost certainly won't be. But it *is* very do-able.

There are a couple of Jedi Mind Tricks, otherwise known as life hacks, that you can use to make things a little easier. Most of them are psychological in nature, and once you start to incorporate them into your writing life, you'll be surprised at just how powerful and effective they can be.

Getting Paid to Write

Did you ever have a job you really didn't like? Yes, me too. Most people have taken a job at some point in their lives that didn't exactly fill them with joy; sometimes, it can grow into something you actively loathe.

In the worst case scenario, it somehow manages to become a career.

At the time I first began to seriously contemplate writing a book, I had one of those jobs. I was working as a computer network engineer for a major I.T. company, one which shall remain nameless. When I first started working there in the late 1990s, it was a terrific place to be. Great people, plenty of opportunities for travel and education, and fulfilling technical work. I loved it.

Slowly, all of that began to change. The company started to outsource more and more jobs overseas, 'leaning' the workforce (the actual term they used) and getting those who remained behind to do much more with far less. I worked the night shift, through personal preference. It was quieter and gave me the opportunity to read and study once my work was done for the evening. Besides, how could a ghost hunter turn down a schedule that was officially known as 'working graveyards?'

The urge to write something more than the occasional short story had been getting stronger and stronger for quite some time before I finally sat down and did something about it.

I spent a while pondering the question of just what, exactly, I was going to write about. As a lifelong aficionado of all things paranormal, I knew that this was going to be my overall topic, but that was a pretty broad definition.

Finally, I came to the conclusion that I was best suited to writing a 'how to' sort of book, teaching the reader about some of the tools and techniques I used for investigating an alleged haunting. I had been involved with paranormal field research for almost twenty years at that point, and figured that I had a picked up a few worthwhile teaching points along the way.

After my work was over and done with for the evening, I fired up my personal laptop, opened a new Microsoft Word document (to which I gave the working title '*How to be a Ghost Hunter*') and began to type.

About five minutes and fifty words later, doubt set in. Hard.

Who the hell was *I* to write a book, I suddenly demanded of myself. I wasn't remotely qualified. I had never written one before. Every line I typed looked painfully amateurish when I read it back, almost cringe-worthy when compared to the work of other authors I'd read. I was deluding myself to think that *I* could write anything publishable…

…wasn't I?

I didn't know it at the time, but this was the voice of my own inner critic, the return of our friend Steven Pressfield's Resistance. It came damned close to talking me out of ever writing another word. Far easier, it seemed to whisper, to give up on my pretensions of getting published, and just kick back with a good book that somebody else had written instead. That way, I was in no danger of being rejected. My time wouldn't be wasted. My feelings wouldn't get hurt. Most importantly (for Resistance is completely rooted in ego) my ego would be protected, safe from injury.

That voice is a liar, dear reader. It is an absolute bastard, not least because it sounds so very *reasonable*.

You need to train yourself to ignore it, no matter how seductive it may sound.

If I had listened to it, I would never have had a writing career.

Feeling the need to step away from the keyboard for a bit, I went outside for a late-night stroll. It was a beautiful, cloudless night, with a glorious Rocky Mountain sky full of stars stretching far over my head. I ended up walking for a couple of miles around the campus perimeter, fighting an inner battle against my own doubts and fears.

Finally, after wrestling with that awful voice for a few days, I hit upon a little mental trick that seemed to come right out of nowhere. My ultimate goal was to become a published writer, I reasoned, and published writers get paid for their time. One of my biggest fears was that I would write a 50,000+-word book, only to have it rejected out of hand by any publishers or agents that I sent it to. Not only would I feel like a total failure, but I would have wasted hours of my time, with only the egg on my face to show for it.

But, I thought to myself, *what if I wrote the entire book on company time?* The company gave me an hour-long lunch break every day. How much writing could I do in the space of an hour?

Excited at the prospect, I went back to my desk, set a timer running, and began to write. When the hour was up, I had written close to 500 words of semi-usable material – it was something like 478 words, give or take.

Mentally, I ran the numbers. If I wrote 500 words each night, that would give me 2,000 words per week. Multiply that by 30 weeks, and I've have written 60,000 words — all of it on the company's time, and also on the company's dime, while still getting my job done.

In other words, I would be a *paid* writer. If the book was rejected, then so what? All that I would have lost was a few lunch hours, but that was one hundred percent 'dead time' anyway. The company owned it. I was burning *their* time, not my own.

There and then, I resolved to sit down and write for an hour each night that I worked, eating at my keyboard rather than going out for a walk. After a few nights of doing this, something very interesting started to happen. My word count slowly began to creep upward. I was hitting 600, 700, often

800 words per hour, sometimes even making it to 1,000.

It took me four months to write that first book.

The publisher rejected it straight away, but I didn't care. They would end up buying my second book, which was also written on my lunch hour at work. That book — the aforementioned *In Search of the Paranormal* — marked the start of my journey as a professional writer. It would never have been written if I hadn't been able to trick myself into getting its first draft finished.

You Don't <u>Have</u> to Write

That might seem like a strange thing for me to say, particularly in light of the fact that I've been extolling the necessity of hitting your word count each and every day, but please bear with me.

I am, and always have been, a massive *Star Wars* fan. In fact, I've been looking for an excuse to insert a *Star Wars* reference into this book for the last 17,000 words or so, and now, *finally,* here's my chance!

Remember that great scene in *Return of the Jedi* when Luke Skywalker confronts the Force ghost of Obi Wan Kenobi and demands to know why the old Jedi Master had claimed that Darth Vader had betrayed and murdered Luke's father? Luke has since learned differently, having his hand cut off in the process: Darth Vader **IS** his father.

"Luke, you're going to find that many of the truths we cling to depend greatly on our own point of view," Obi Wan tells the fledgling Jedi. (I think I now owe George Lucas — sorry, Disney — a dollar for quoting that line).

The physical act of sitting down in a chair and starting to write can sometimes feel like a chore. Even if you really love doing it once the process finally gets rolling, actually starting out can be a challenge. There are a million other things competing for your time and attention, not least the desire to just sit back and entertain yourself, rather than add more 'work' to your already overloaded day.

There's something about that word — *work* — that snarls up the human brain. It has negative connotations for most people. It's not something that they necessarily enjoy doing. I served as a volunteer firefighter for fifteen years, and loved pretty much every minute of it. I would respond to emergency calls directly from home if the incident was big enough, and work an overnight shift or two at the firehouse every week, helping to staff a first-due fire engine as a firefighter-paramedic.

There were also paid firefighters working on the department. Many were volunteers who had chosen to make firefighting their career. The great majority of them still loved what they did, but one or two did not. After talking to them at length around the dinner table for many years, I learned something interesting: the ones that complained the most, the ones that seemed to begrudge being there, were most often paid firefighters who had started to think of it as 'work.'

Somewhere along the way, they had lost the joy and passion that they had started out with as raw recruits in the fire academy. They were no longer choosing to be there at the firehouse; they *had* to be there, because that was how they put food on the table and paid their mortgage at the end of the month. It had begun as a passion and somewhere along the way, they had mentally downgraded it to the status of a job.

There are days when writing feels the same way. I'll sit down at my keyboard and feel all of my motivation to write slipping away like grains of sand through my fingers.

That's when I change my frame of reference, choosing to adopt a different point of view. It's a deliberate act, one that requires conscious effort on my part. Before sitting down, I remind myself of one very important thing:

I don't *have* to write.

I *get* to write.

Writing isn't a chore to be gotten over and done with as quickly as possible, like loading the dishwasher or taking out the garbage. It's actually a pleasure and a privilege to perform, if you only choose to see it that way. I remind myself that once the book is finished and hits general release, readers are going to do me the very great honor of handing over some of their hard-earned money in exchange for the right to read it. That's a huge deal to me, and something that a writer should never take lightly. Time is the one resource that none of us can earn more of, and therefore, by definition, the most precious.

To think that somebody is going to spend some of their irreplaceable time reading the words that you now labor over, should always be foremost in your mind.

Yes, writing can feel like work sometimes, but it's not exactly breaking rocks in a chain gang, is it? You're there by choice, choosing to share your vision with the world. Nobody's forcing you to do it, so you may as well learn to have fun with it and learn to love the process.

I promise you that it's one hundred percent worth it.

CHAPTER EIGHT

Resistance

I've already mentioned the concept of Resistance, as put forward by Steven Pressfield in his exceptional manifesto for fledgling writers, *The War of Art*. Resistance, inertia, or whatever else you want to call it, can be an absolute bastard, but make no mistake: you can beat it if you are willing to put in the effort.

Unfortunately, it's not going to be easy, and there are no shortcuts. In the same way that losing weight is simple but not easy (burn more calories than you consume, period — something I continually fail to do) the answer to beating resistance is equally straightforward. Here's the secret:

Turn up every day. Sit yourself down at the keyboard.

Write until you hit your word count.

Do the same thing again tomorrow.

And the next day.

And the next.

Wash. Rinse. Repeat. Until your book is done.

That's it. That's all it takes.

Simple, right? But not easy.

You have to learn to push aside that insidious mental voice, the one that is telling you your writing sucks, that it's absolutely terrible. It's trying to get you to believe that nobody will want to read what you have written, because you're just not good enough. I still struggle with that voice on a daily basis. It's talking to me right now, in fact, as I write these words (though not in a literal sense). It's been with me since word one of book number one, and will probably be whispering its bile in my ear until the day I die.

You're not good enough.

Your work is shit.

Nobody wants to read the crap you're writing.

Please pardon my language, but you need to tell that voice to go and fuck itself. In the strongest possible terms.

It's lying to you. It's lying to me. I can prove it, just by looking up at the shelves in my office. There are seventeen books lined up in a row there, all with my name on the spine and on the cover. Disregarding the self-published books, there are still titles by *four* different publishing houses, all of whose editors somehow judged my work to be of sufficiently professional quality for them to buy and then put out into the world.

Yet still the voice persists. It's trying to undermine me,

and it will also try to undermine you. Sometimes the voice is loud, sometimes it is quiet, but it is always *there,* an inner critic that wants nothing more than to sabotage all of your efforts.

For all of my fellow *Star Wars* fans out there, this is the path to the dark side: "Quicker, easier, more seductive…" It wants you to give up, to quit. To not finish. Your own ego is sabotaging you because it fears the consequences of what may happen when you publish your book. There'll inevitably be some disappointment and criticism, no matter how good or bad the finished product turns out to be, and the ego *hates* to be criticized.

Hence, Resistance, and that damnable voice.

You have to shut it out (it will never shut up) long enough to get your work done. Once you start writing your book, you don't stop. For *anything.*

Your sole task is power on through to the finish without getting derailed. No matter what happens, keep writing. Day in, day out, hit that word count, by hook or by crook. Advance your total number of words written each and every day.

"But what if my writing really *does* suck?"

The truth is, if this is your first attempt at writing (or your tenth, for that matter, or your fiftieth) then it probably *does*. And that's okay. It's absurd to expect somebody to master the craft of writing the first time out. It's a process of continual learning, where the best teacher is trial and error. There aren't any short cuts. You have to put down tens of thousands, if not *hundreds* of thousands of words, to become truly proficient at this craft. (I'm still working on it).

But that's part of what makes writing so rewarding. Each book you write is going to be better than the last; a little sharper, clearer, more coherent. They'll grow increasingly polished and refined as you become better at your craft. That's true of any profession. The more time and effort you put in, the slicker the end result becomes. I'm a better paramedic now than I was ten years ago — though I still have a lot to learn — because I've assessed hundreds of patients in that span of time. The same holds true where my writing is concerned.

A word about perfectionism: it can only hinder you in the early stages. This is your first draft of at least two, possibly more. Don't allow yourself to get caught in the weeds when it comes to the minutiae. Perhaps your sentence structure is looking a little bit clunky. Maybe you know there's a better word to use than the one you've chosen, but you just can't quite put your finger on it. Don't spend time trying to tweak and fine-tune, or searching for the perfect phrase. Write and move on.

You're in a race to the finish. What are you racing against? That voice. Resistance. Inertia. Your ego. Call it what you will, it's the drag factor that wants nothing more than to see you fail, to call it quits and give up.

Once you get to the very last page and type the words 'The End,' it's over. Your race is won. Then you can breathe again. There's a huge, almost palpable sense of relief when the first draft of your manuscript is all done and dusted. There's no longer that long, seemingly endless road of blank white space in front of you. You've hit the end of the track, and it's all downhill from there.

It doesn't matter if you've written the literary equivalent of a steaming turd, something so rank that it could curdle milk at fifty paces. The crucial thing is that you have *finished*. Now you have something to work with.

"Arrakis teaches the attitude of the knife — chopping off what's incomplete and saying: 'Now it's complete because it ended here.'" — From *Dune,* by Frank Herbert.

CHAPTER NINE

The Edit

You've finished your first draft. Congratulations, Padawan — you've written your first book.

YOU. HAVE. WRITTEN. A. *BOOK!*

Pat yourself on the back, because you bloody well deserve it. Your race to the finish is over, and you *won.* Resistance didn't beat you; you kicked its ass six ways to Sunday.

Bravo, you. My hat goes off to you for simply getting this far. Countless would-be writers have failed to make it to the place where you now stand. They fell at the wayside and chose to give up. But not you. You were made of sterner stuff.

Again, bravo.

So, what comes next?

Put your manuscript away somewhere for a week or so. Print it out, stick it in your desk drawer, and then walk away. Give yourself a little space from it. If you're feeling pumped and super-motivated, feel free to start making notes and working on an outline for your second book; but what you must under no circumstances do, is to rush this one out into the world before it's ready, half-baked and tepid.

It's not unheard of for first-time writers to self-publish their first attempt at writing a book without getting it properly edited or proofed. They usually just want to just get something out there. Unfortunately, the something they get out there often contains multiple grammatical and typographical errors. In more than a few books, you'll see sentences in which Words Are Capitalized That Should Not Be.

It's unfortunate, because as you'll learn when we start talking about how you'll go about establishing your own brand, you only get one shot at making a first impression with readers. If the product they purchase from you looks anything less than professional, the chances are good that they'll never give you a second opportunity to impress them. Which is a shame, because somewhere in there, hidden within the sloppiness, there's probably a great story to be told.

I hate to say this, but sometimes you'll have better luck polishing a turd (a dull book that's professionally presented) than putting out something good that's presented scruffily. As chefs like to say about food, "The first bite is taken with the eye."

When you've finished writing your book, you will probably experience an overwhelming temptation to release it straight away. It's totally understandable. All that hard work, and you'll want to put it into the hands of readers as soon as humanly possible.

Resist that urge.

After a week or so — no less, though longer is fine — come back to your project and look at it with a fresh eye. Read through each chapter in order. Use a printed manuscript and not a computer screen, because you'll be doing this with a red pen in your hand.

Read slowly and carefully, as a reader might. Your eye has a tendency to see what your brain *thinks* it wrote. You'll be shocked at how many times you wrote something along the lines of: "I wanted to sea what happened next," or "There car broke down." Spell check usually won't catch the SEA and THERE/THEIR errors because they are not spelling errors; they're grammatical in nature. Sometimes, grammar-checking software will catch these howlers; sometimes it won't.

A good rule of thumb is to write fast and read slow.

This first edit is also where you'll pick up on the clunky sentence structuring that we talked about earlier. In the early stages of your writing career, you're still forming and developing your own writing style. As a product of the British education system from the 1970s and 1980s, which came with a host of mandatory English classes, I tend to write very formally. In my working life as a paramedic chief, I regularly write emails to doctors, managers, and other medical professionals, which tend to be of a formal nature. It's therefore a bit of a struggle for me to write conversationally in a book such as this one. Sometimes I succeed, sometimes I don't. My writing style is constantly evolving, which is a good thing.

Just because a sentence is grammatically correct, however, doesn't mean that it will read well. Take a look at the following two sentences:

"The dark, shadowy old manor house was bleak and crumbling, and looked rather eerie from what I could see when we pulled up outside; as I walked around the place, a vague, almost indefinable sense of dread began to well up inside me, perhaps foreshadowing the events of the night to come."

"I'd seen horror movies that were set in houses like this."

Each of those descriptions is valid. One is a heck of a lot simpler than the other. It can be argued that the first does a better job of setting the scene, explaining the creepy atmosphere of the location in far more detail; yet at the same time, the second sentence gets our adventure off and running in just eleven words.

Neither is intrinsically better than the other. Which one best fits your writing style — richly evocative, or clean and simplistic? There are no strictly right answers here. There is only the right answer *for you.*

Take a red pen to sentences in the book that seem out of place. Highlight typos, spelling errors, and grammatical errors wherever you find them. Think of the editing process as being something analogous to a sculptor chipping away at his or her masterpiece. The broad outlines were hewn out of the block of stone during the early stages. Now it's time for some refinement, subtracting a little here, changing a little there, in order to better serve the overall aesthetic.

A good thing to remember about editing is that, generally speaking, you should be taking away, rather than adding more. It's rare that my second draft, after it has gone through the editing process, is longer than the first. I tend to write longer first drafts very quickly, and then cut away some of the excess bloat afterward. The overall structure of the book shouldn't change, unless there's something drastically wrong with it that you happen to discover on the first proper read through.

This is your chance to fix any of those issues you glossed over when you were charging through the first draft. You can edit at your leisure; the pressure to get the thing finished is off your shoulders now. There's no longer any rush, because the fear and uncertainty of reaching the finish line is now gone. You can breathe easy and go at your own pace.

When you reach the end for the second time, you should be left with a leaner, crisper manuscript. Once that's done, the book should be structurally sound *and* hang together well. Now it's time to have another set of eyes go over it.

You always want your book to be the most professional product that it can possibly be, especially if it's your first (remember, this can make or break your opportunity to build a potential readership). That means it's time to look for the services of a line editor and/or a copy editor.

Line and Copy Editing

The terms 'line editor' and 'copy editor' are sometimes used interchangeably. This makes sense, because there is often a degree of overlap between their areas of responsibility.

A line editor is looking at the overall quality of the work. They're not as interested in the nuts and bolts aspects such as typos and spelling mistakes; the line editor is going to assess your manuscript carefully and tell you whether you've written a coherent book, with a solid, logical structure. If you've written a piece of fiction, they'll let you know whether, in their opinion, it successfully tells a compelling story, one which makes sense and isn't confusing. Do characters suddenly turn up out of nowhere, for example?

Jeff was six feet tall and two hundred pounds of pure muscle. Sighing, he ran a hand through his short, black hair. It was slicked with sweat. He wiped a muscular forearm across his sweat-soaked forehead, brushing back a stray lock of close-cut, raven-dark hair.

A line editor might point out the redundancy of repeatedly telling the reader about Jeff's muscularity, the shortness of his hair, the fact that it's black, and his sweatiness. The writer might not catch these things during the initial writing process, and can sometimes miss them while working on the second draft.

If your book is non-fiction, on the other hand, the line

editor may tell you whether your writing style is clumsy or ham-handed. Does your prose clearly and accurately convey your point to the reader, or have you written a muddled, confusing mess that is difficult to make head or tail of?

The line editor's input can be invaluable. It can mean the difference between putting out a compelling book or releasing a sloppy morass of sheer confusion.

A copy editor, on the other hand, is checking the quality of your manuscript. They are the ones who will find all of the glaring typos that you missed during your read through. They'll also look for inconsistencies in the text. This is a bit like the role of the continuity specialist in the TV and film world, whose job it is to make sure that characters are wearing the same clothing from scene to scene, and that scars don't suddenly switch from one side of the face to the other (Rian Johnson, I'm looking at you).

Good copy editors are worth their weight in gold, and they seem to be becoming something of an endangered species. Have you noticed just how many of the A-list novels these days, the stuff put out by major publishing houses and the biggest names in fiction, have a shocking number of typos in them? By my reckoning, it's a *lot*. That never used to happen, but it's becoming increasingly common. Have readers just become used to it and gotten more accepting of such errors? Considering the price of a hardback book these days, they shouldn't have to. Whatever the case may be, you don't want your book to be counted among them.

For the non-fiction writer, line or copy editors will keep an eye on some of your factual information. They should catch the error when you write something like: *The Second World War began on December 17th, 1940, when the Germans launched a surprise attack on Pearl Harbor.* (Although, if your understanding of history is genuinely *that* bad, you may want to pick another topic to write about).

You may find line editors who also offer most of the same services that a copy editor does, and vice versa. Either way, I strongly recommend that you pay a line or copy editor if you can possibly afford one. I once had a very embarrassing experience when I wrote a book about a haunted inn and its connection to the American Civil War. I was writing about the Battle of Gettysburg, one of the subjects that I'm extremely passionate and quite knowledgeable about. I have walked the field at Gettysburg numerous times, and used a wealth of primary and secondary research material during the writing of the book.

There was just one problem. At a couple of points in the

book, I referred to the battle as having taken place in June of 1863. It actually took place in July. Throughout 95% of the manuscript, I had the correct dates. That doesn't matter. When I did my read-through, my eyes saw what my brain *thought* it had told my hands to write: the word *July*.

Like an idiot (this was one of my earlier books) I went against my own advice, and declined to submit the book to a copy editor, figuring that I'd save some money. More fool me. My proof reader missed the errors too, which is totally understandable; she's not particularly well-versed in the chronology of the Civil War, and focused most of her attention on looking for typos and formatting errors, of which there were several.

The book duly made it into print and got some great reviews. I was pleased with the positive reader response, and moved on to my next book project.

Then the sky fell (alright, not *literally*, but really shitty Amazon reviews can sure make it feel like that sometimes).

There's nothing new here except a lot of amateur typos, the review began. *Besides the annoying typos (It seems no one proof read this book before publication; for example the author repeatedly refers to the second day of the Gettysburg Battle as "June 2") this book repeats what you find in other, better, books.*

Ouch.

I'll talk about the way in which to deal with negative reviews later on, but one of the cardinal rules put out there by wiser authors is that you should never, ever respond to them. Generally speaking, I tend to agree; anybody who paid to read your book has a right to dislike it, or even to hate it with a burning passion. But in this case, the criticism leveled at the book wasn't inaccurate. In my opinion, it *was* just a little bit overblown — the book was hardly *riddled* with typos — but the reviewer did highlight a genuine error in the manuscript, one that I immediately corrected in both the digital and print editions. I then wrote them a response note on the Amazon website, thanking them for letting me know about the problem with my book.

They didn't deign to reply, but that's okay. I was in the wrong. I should have gotten the book professionally line or copy edited.

Don't make my mistake.

Get an editor.

Some freelancers advertise their services on websites such as Fiverr.com or Freelancer.com, to name just two. Be sure to check their references and read any reviews left by former clients before engaging their services. A good editor/proofreader may not come cheap, but they are truly worth their weight in gold.

CHAPTER TEN

Test Readers

Now that your book has been line/copy-edited, it's not a bad idea to put it in front of a few trusted test readers in order to solicit some feedback.

I wouldn't suggest enlisting your mum, dad, or significant other. They aren't going to want to hurt your feelings by offering up any truly pointed criticism. Although getting a pat on the head from a loved one is always nice, it isn't all that useful when it comes down to spotting any real problems with your writing.

A better option might be asking for volunteers from amongst your list of Facebook friends, or joining one of the many writing support groups that proliferate out there on the Internet. Strangers are (hopefully) more likely to be objective, and tell you what they *really* think of your book.

One word of caution here: never ask for criticism unless you are truly ready to receive it. It can be hard to hear that your precious little darling, the literary masterpiece that you've been slaving over for months, is anything less than perfect. You must brace yourself and prepare to be told exactly that.

Sometimes, the criticism you'll get isn't particularly useful.

"I just didn't like it."

"I'm sorry to hear that. Why not?"

"Oh, I'm not really sure…"

Take criticism like that with a huge grain of salt.

On the other hand, the test reader that tells you they couldn't really get into the book because the first half was a little too slow, is doing you a huge favor. This is doubly true if you hear the same thing from multiple people. It gives you an opportunity to go back and revisit the manuscript with a more critical eye of your own.

Is the first half of the book *really* too slow? Be honest with yourself. Do you need to inject some excitement, make some edits, or just generally pick up the pace? That kind of criticism is pure gold, no matter how much it might sting. Be sure to give it the serious consideration that it deserves.

Whatever else you do, don't just shrug it off.

Stick a Fork in it

At the risk of sounding like a hypocrite, there's no such thing as perfection when it comes to the process of publishing.

Yes, I know that I've been beating the "banish all the errors" drum so far, but the truth is that even after a read-through, a line edit, a copy edit, and a spell in front of your test readers, mistakes will *still* creep into your book somehow. It's inevitable. All you can do is maximize them as best you possibly can.

Maximize? Crap! I meant minimize. *Minimize!* See?

The enemy of good is perfect. Once your book has been through several different sets of hands, and you have incorporated any resulting changes into the manuscript, know when to call it a day. When all's said and done, once you've weeded out as many errors as you can reasonably find, good enough is good enough.

Set it aside again.

Know when to stick a fork in it, and call it done.

CHAPTER ELEVEN

Choose Your Path

At this stage of the game, you'd be forgiven for thinking that the hard part is over and done with.

Your book has now been outlined, written, edited, proof-read, and test-read. It's time to take a running jump at the next big hurdle: getting that sucker published.

I'm not going to lie to you: it's a daunting task. It's difficult. It's frustrating, sometimes to the point of making you want to quit.

But it's also do-able.

When things start to get difficult, don't allow yourself to forget that.

Ten years ago, you would have had no choice but to attempt to weave your way through the minefield that is traditional publishing. Literary agents and acquisition editors were the gatekeepers that you had to either appease or defeat (and good luck with *that*) before your book would ever see the light of day.

Thankfully, things have changed since then — for the better. Yes, those traditional gatekeepers are still there, and in some cases, it may still be worth your while to try to deal with them…but their way is no longer the only way. Thanks to the explosive popularity of self-publishing, we now have a level playing field.

This is both good and bad.

Just take a look through the Amazon Kindle library and you'll see what I mean. There are more books out there than ever before. The sheer amount of reading material available is nothing short of overwhelming. Tens of millions of titles, all of them vying for the attention of a potential reading market – one that is utterly spoiled for choice.

Talk about a double-edged sword! While your book has every right to sit on the digital shelf alongside all those others, it is ridiculously easy for it to get lost within the background noise, one tiny voice among millions, crying out for somebody to read it. It's why so many books go unread, slowly sinking their way down into the depths of the Amazon rankings chart, selling — if the author is lucky — a handful of copies each month, at most.

It's even harder to find an audience now than it has been in the past. Harder, but *not* impossible. A number of my books are available for sale in my local bookstore, for example, and also at the city library. I doubt that this would be the case if I had confined myself entirely to self-publishing. Having a traditional publisher was of *enormous* benefit when it came to breaking into those corners of the reading market.

The lion's share of this coming section of the book will be devoted to the finer points of self-publishing versus traditional publishing. I'll help you figure out which option — traditional (trad), self-published (indie), or hybrid — is right for you, by discussing the pros and cons of each, and will then assist you in devising a strategy for success.

Let's start with the old guard, shall we?

CHAPTER TWELVE

Traditional Publishing

Pros

It is commonly believed that, for a writer, one of the biggest selling points of going down the path of traditional publishing is that you only have to *write* the book. Proofing, editing, printing, distribution, and promotion are all handled by somebody else. That may be somewhat true, or at least, it *used* to be that way (and still is, for the higher-echelon authors whose sales figures number in the millions) but the truth, as is so often the case, is actually somewhat different.

Here's how things *really* work when I write a book for a traditional publisher.

Firstly, I have to create a proposal. This usually consists of an 'elevator pitch,' just a paragraph or two that manage to encapsulate the essence of the book in a clear and concise way; a basic outline, much like the one I've already shown you how to create for your own book; and three full-length sample chapters. If you're already a known quantity to the publisher, having successfully submitted work to them in the past, then they'll sometimes relax and be a little more flexible where the sample chapters are concerned. After all, you have a proven track record, so they already *know* that you can write to a professional standard. If this is your first pitch to them, however, then they'll want proof that you're capable of generating a decent amount of publishable material.

In addition to all of that, there is often a requirement for the writer to submit some sort of marketing plan. This is essentially your attempt to prove to the publishing house that there is a market for your book. What other titles are similar, and will therefore act as its direct competition? Who is the target audience for your book? Do you already have any kind of pre-built readership that you can bring to the table?

If you're a first-time author, the answer to most of these questions will usually be "no" or "not much." You may have wondered how certain 'celebrities,' some of whom are barely even literate, can land themselves six and seven-figure book deals. The answer is, of course, that they come with a built-in fanbase. If you happen to have a following on Twitter that numbers in the millions, then getting a publisher will be an absolute piece of cake. Book sales are pretty much guaranteed (at least, enough that they will almost certainly make their money back, and perhaps even generate a little profit on top) so publishing houses are far more likely to take the plunge where a celebrity is concerned. It doesn't matter whether the aforementioned celeb can actually *write;* that's what ghost writers are for (no, not me — the other kind).

It therefore stands to reason that you, the never-before-published first timer, are going to have to get by on your talent and hard work — not to mention a fair bit of luck.

A word about literary agents: getting an agent to represent you also has its benefits and drawbacks — and can be equally difficult, if not more so, than dealing directly with a publishing house. For one thing, an agent will often want to see the entire manuscript before agreeing to take you on as a client, which means you will have to complete it and get your edits all done prior to submission.

Do you actually *need* an agent? Well, that's a big gray area. An agent can do some very beneficial things for you, the most important being to shop your manuscript around to traditional publishing houses both large and small. This vastly increases your chances of getting your book in front of people who might actually be willing to publish it, rather than lost in the depths of the never-ending slush pile (more on that later). They will also help negotiate film and TV rights, should you happen to have a stroke of massive good fortune and somehow manage to get Hollywood interested in your work.

The downside is that an agent will take a hefty chunk of any profits that you make on the book, usually somewhere in the realm of 15% but possibly more. I know many successful writers that have taken a cold, hard look at the idea of getting an agent, only to decide that it just isn't necessary for them. Dealing directly with the publisher, without having to go through an intermediary, is sometimes a better deal for the writer. It also helps that they don't have to give up that extra 15%.

If you're going to attempt to get an agent, this is usually achieved by sending a query letter to one that you feel would be a good fit for you. To be absolutely honest, dealing with an agent is not within my area of expertise, because I have never actually had to do it myself. I have always dealt directly with my publishers, and don't foresee that changing any time soon. I'd rather give you minimal advice on the subject than bad advice, so instead, I'll refer you to one of the numerous books available on the subject, if this is the route that you ultimately decide to pursue.

Assuming for a moment that your proposal is accepted,

you're still not out of the woods. A contract will be signed and you'll be paid an advance, which can be anything from a few hundred to a few thousand dollars – although an increasing number of smaller publishing houses are now paying no advances at all to their writers.

Once the book is finished, the publisher is almost guaranteed to want you to make some changes. This often occurs after they have what's called a 'vision meeting' (or something similar) in which a number of key players at the publishing house get a chance to review your manuscript. Depending on the size of the organization, this could involve anyone from the acquisition editor, a representative of the marketing department, all the way on up to senior management and the owner of the business.

The purpose of this meeting is to determine how best to make your book sell. Sometimes, they are going to ask you to make changes that you do not agree with. Make no mistake — now that you have signed a contract with them, the publisher's 'suggestions' are nothing of the sort. They're *mandates.* The publisher owns the book now, not you, and the writer ignores these 'suggestions' at their peril.

Credit where credit's due: I should point out that the people who work at publishing houses sell books for a living. They know which factors separate a barn burner of a project from a polished turd (at least, they *should*), and have a vested interest in making your book a success. With that being said, sometimes the changes they ask for can really chafe.

In the early days of my writing career, I received several pages worth of those requested changes from an editor. Some were relatively minor, such as the removal of a sentence or two here and there; no big deal. Others were significantly bigger, requiring me to cut entire chapters or drastically rewrite them because somebody at the meeting didn't like what I had written.

A case in point would be one of my paranormal non-fiction books. I had written a chapter which involved a self-proclaimed psychic, a lady who was quite obviously disturbed and delusional. To give you some idea, she had written an email accusing me of having deliberately opened up a portal to Hell during one of my investigations. A bunch of ghostly miners were supposedly coming through this portal and were sexually harassing her — whenever she took a shower at home. (I had never even been within ten miles of this lady's house, and even if I believed in the concept of Hell, I wouldn't have the slightest idea of how to open up a portal to the place!)

To be fair, in the chapter I had written, I was rather scathing of the claims this lady was making. While I'm not anti-psychic by any means (having worked with some wonderful ones), I do believe that *some* of those who claim to have those kinds of abilities are deluded at best, and intentionally fraudulent at worst. When I said as much in print, the publisher took me to task: "Just *who* do you think the audience for your paranormal book is, Richard?" This entire section of the chapter needed to go, the editor demanded. There was to be no negotiation on that point.

At first, I was pretty steamed about it, but with the benefit of hindsight, I can see that the editor was making a valid point. People who read books about the paranormal generally don't want to read about bad psychics being debunked — they want to hear about the genuine article. Many of those readers hold similar beliefs, and that particular section of the book could easily have alienated them. My words came across as tarring all psychic mediums with the same brush. What a great way to piss off a large section of the potential readership I was hoping to build.

In my opinion, the old saying that we need to respect the beliefs of all people is just not true. We don't. What we do need to do is respect *their right to hold those beliefs, and to freely express them.* In other words, it's okay to criticize ideas and concepts; it is not okay to ridicule and belittle the people who cling to them. In this particular case, the editor's vision notes were right on the money, and I was given a much-needed education in how not to anger the people who might want to buy my book…and how not to be a dick.

Sometimes, yet another set of fresh, objective, and above all, *professional* eyes on your finished manuscript turns out to be a very good thing indeed. All publishers have a vested interest in their products selling well, and that definitely works to the writer's advantage.

P.R. and Marketing

Even before your book hits the shelves, the publisher's marketing and P.R. department should be working on your behalf to drum up some buzz. This will take a variety of different forms.

P.R. people are well-connected with the media, and will pro-actively contact their counterparts at TV and radio stations, magazines, websites, and also reach out to bloggers and other social influencers, working to get you and your book in front of a wider audience.

Due to their subject matter, the majority of my traditionally-published books hit the market during the months leading up to Halloween. This is a no-brainer really; ghost stories, whether fact or fiction, tend to sell more copies in the month of October than at any other time of the year. That makes the September-October-November period a natural sales window for the sort of stuff I write, and the kind of things my publishers specialize in.

Trad publishers like to put a book out there for pre-order several months before its actual release date. That permits interested readers to order it in advance and receive it on the day of publication. The marketing department begins ramping up their efforts about six weeks to a month before the book's scheduled release date. Requests for media interviews start landing in the author's inbox at around the same time.

A good PR professional will arrange for the author to give presentations and attend signings at reputable book stores. Their design and print shop will produce promotional materials such as book marks, flyers, banners, and post cards to help raise awareness. If they're *really* prepared to push the boat out, the author might even be lucky enough to get an ad paid for in Bookbub, arguably the premium book promotional service in the United States.

Not too shabby, all things considered.

For a writer, there are few more satisfying feelings in life than to walk into your local branch of Barnes and Noble, Waterstones, or whatever your favorite book store is, and see your name on the cover of a book sitting proudly on one of the shelves. (If it isn't sitting proudly, it takes almost super-human self-control not to place your baby front and center on one of the displays).

It's hard to deny that being traditionally published garners one a certain cachet. In the world of publishing, as everywhere else, there is a degree of snobbery to be found. It isn't necessarily unwarranted, either. In a day and age where somebody can bash out a few thousand words of poorly-written prose, slap a plain text cover on it, and call it a book, there's something to be said for the knowledge that the title you've paid hard-earned money for was vetted by a professional team of editors. That's what a product which comes out of a publishing house promises: a sense of pedigree and respectability, based upon the unspoken promise that the quality of the book meets an accepted professional standard.

Cons

Contrary to a popular misconception, the traditionally-published author's work isn't quite done once they turn in their manuscript. You *do* still have to proof your own galleys, for example; as has already been mentioned, even the best proofreaders and editors still make mistakes.

A case in point: in one of my own trad books, which was published very early in my career, I had cause to write about President Roosevelt, and his place in American history. Nothing particularly challenging there, you might think, but nevertheless, I managed to screw things up royally. There were, of course, *two* President Roosevelts — Theodore, and Franklin Delano. I picked the wrong one. I was up late and writing while I was fairly tired, cranking out my daily word count. That's no excuse at all, but it *is* the explanation for how I managed to let such a rookie error get into my manuscript in the first place. It should have been caught by me during the read-through (it wasn't) and the line/copy editors at the publishing house (it wasn't) or their editorial test readers (nope).

At the end of the day, the responsibility for the gaffe lies with me. I signed off on those final galleys, which then went straight to print. It taught me a very hard-earned and embarrassing lesson: Nobody, and I really do mean *nobody*, is as invested in your book as you are. Not the editor; not the publisher; not the marketing department. Nobody.

Yes, the publishing house wants to sell as many copies of your book as possible, but ultimately, it's just one product among many in their book catalog. If your book is released to little or modest fanfare, and promptly vanishes without a trace, they are ultimately going to shrug their shoulders and move on to the next writer's work. In terms of long-term consequences, a failed book title just makes it all the more likely that they will never offer you a contract again…ever. You'll be perceived – perhaps rightly – as a losing proposition.

It is therefore incumbent upon you as the writer to put as much time, effort, and sweat into making your project as good as it can possibly be. In the self-publishing world, good enough is often good enough (within reason) — after all, you are your own boss, and you're not likely to fire yourself. It's a different story in the world of traditional publishing.

One of the biggest drawbacks when it comes to going trad is

the total lack of control the writer has over the finished product.

Looking back at the covers on the stuff I've written for various publishing houses over the years, I've noticed that there's a pretty wide range of quality on display. Some of them are downright superb, whereas others, well…let's just say that they're a little underwhelming, or at least not quite representative of the theme and contents of the book. I mean no disrespect to the graphic designers and artists, all of whom put their very best efforts into designing those covers, but a couple of them just don't quite fit.

While the publishers have always been polite enough to solicit my opinion on the covers before they are released, on a couple of occasions (with two different publishing houses) I suggested changes that I felt would greatly benefit book sales. In the first case, I suggested that what I thought was a somewhat bland cover ought perhaps to have something to spice it up a little — maybe an image of the haunted location itself, with a mysterious, shadowy figure or two lurking nearby.

My suggestion was politely rebuffed. I shrugged and moved on to my next project, not feeling overly perturbed by it. That's just the way the cookie crumbles, I reasoned, and tried not to let it bother me.

The second example was a little different. My heart sank when I saw the proposed cover of the book that had been emailed to me in the form of a PDF. The book I had written was a dark, frightening story, set in a location that was extremely creepy. Much to my chagrin, what the graphic designer delivered was something far better suited to the contents of a period romance novel. There was absolutely nothing about this particular cover that conveyed the more terrifying aspects of the haunting I had written about. It wouldn't have looked out of place on the shelf in your local supermarket, right next to the happily-ever-after love stories.

Making sure to be as respectful as I possibly could, I wrote to the publisher and suggested that perhaps a scarier, more intense cover was in order. They, in turn, thanked me politely for my input, and promptly ignored it.

The end result? This particular book received little publicity from the publisher, debuted low in the Amazon charts, and immediately began to sink like a stone. It has not, at the time of writing, earned back its advance, and ranks as one of the weakest-selling titles of my career. It is also the only book I have ever written to have gone out of print.

Fortunately, there was an upside. After a year or two had

passed, the publisher generously allowed the rights for this particular book to revert back to me. When a respectable amount of time has gone by, I will have the opportunity to test my theory out when I re-issue the book with a newly-designed cover in place. My hope is that it will find its target audience more easily the second time around.

Only time will tell.

To some artists, creative control is extremely important. The lack of it can be a deal breaker. If that describes you, then self-publishing is definitely the way to go. For good or for ill, you are the sole driving force behind the way in which your book goes out into the world. The text, length, editing, cover design, and marketing — they're all down to you.

Having a publisher handle some of those things for you can often be a huge load off your shoulders. On the other hand, you might also get more than you bargained for. As I mentioned earlier, once that contract is signed and agreed upon, publishing houses can make any changes to your manuscript that they feel like making, whether you agree with them or not.

This isn't necessarily a bad thing. A case in point: I had

titled my first published work, a volume of paranormal non-fiction experiences, *Fear in the Dark*. I thought it was a pretty decent title, all things being equal. After their vision meeting, the publisher's representative told me that the title of my book had been changed. *Fear in the Dark* was now going to be called *In Search of the Paranormal*.

"There's not a lot of fear in it," the editor explained politely when I enquired about the reason for the change.

After my initial emotional knee-jerk reaction — what did they think they were doing, messing with *my* title? — I finally set eyes on the cover that their graphic designer had put together. I had to eat some humble pie. The cover and the new title not only went very well together, but they also complimented the manuscript perfectly. The publisher had been right, I had been wrong, and I reminded myself once again that the decision had been made by people whose expertise was in selling as many books as possible.

Earning Royalties

No matter whether an author writes as a labor of love, writes because they want to make a living as a wordsmith, or falls somewhere between the two ends of the spectrum, most of us share one thing in common: We would like to get paid for our efforts, and get paid as fairly as possible.

As a writer, you are paid a small sum of money (a 'royalty') for every copy sold. At the very highest levels, authors can make tens of millions. Realistically speaking, however, you're going to make a lot less. *A lot.*

In the world of traditional publishing, it's fairly common for authors to make 10% — 15% of the sale price, although some publishers will pay as little as 7%, particularly if they are one of the smaller presses. Ebook royalties are generally a little higher, which is nice; this reflects the fact that there are minimal production and distribution costs for a digital book, which doesn't have to be printed, bound, and physically shipped to distributors and retailers.

Contrast this with Amazon's Kindle Direct Publishing (KDP), which offers a whopping 60% royalty on paperback sales (minus the costs of printing) and either 35% or 70% on ebooks, depending on which option you choose — more on this later.

It has to be said that not everybody likes Amazon and its business practices, but here are the cold hard facts. As a hybrid author who has released books with multiple trad publishers, I can tell you that my self-publishing income is more than ten times higher than that from my trad books, even when the price of designing my own covers is taken into account.

Ten times.

It's difficult to argue with numbers like that. Unless you truly do not care one whit about the financial aspects of the publishing business, with the current state of the industry, self-publishing offers a deal so competitive that it is almost impossible to beat.

Pricing

It's sometimes difficult to understand the way in which publishers set the prices on their books. The majority of my independently-published (indie) e-books are set at the $3.99-$4.99 price point, for example, which means that I bring in somewhere between $2.75 and $3.50 a copy in royalties. The trad books were being priced around the $10 to $16 mark by their publisher. The end result: I make 25% royalty on the trad ebooks, so while I make more per copy ($2.50 to $4) they sell in much smaller quantities than my indie ebooks do.

My indie books regularly hit several of the top 100-charting Amazon categories on release, with at least one usually being in the top 10. The trad books have frequently been priced out of the market, and end up in the same top 100 lists much less often. After the first week or two of release, when the die-hard fans have picked up their copies (love you guys!) they almost never place in the top 10 again, and usually drop out of the top 100 fairly quickly as well, reappearing only every once in a while – usually around Halloween, or when one of the haunted locations contained in them appears on a TV show such as *Ghost Adventures*.

I'd rather sell 100 ebooks at $3.99 each and get 70% of the profits than sell 10 ebooks at $15 and get 25% each. The numbers simply cannot be argued with, at the end of the day.

(One of my trad publishers seems to have looked at the Amazon sales charts and drawn a similar conclusion, as they have now dropped the price of their ebooks down to the $3—$4 range. That's great for them, as it should translate into more sales, but is arguably worse for their stable of writers, who will now be earning 25% on just 1/4 of the price that they used to sell for).

The freedom to not only price your book at a point which you feel is both fair and attractive, but also to raise and lower it when it suits you for promotional purposes, is worth a great deal to the savvy writer. You give it up completely when you go with a traditional publishing house. Be absolutely sure you're okay with that before you sign a contract with one.

P.R. and Marketing – the downside

We've already talked about the benefits that come with having the P.R. and Marketing department of a publishing house behind you. It's a wonderful thing to have marketing professionals working on your behalf, drumming up publicity and arranging for interviews and media coverage of your work.

Unfortunately, even the most enthusiastic marketing person will only work on your specific book for about three months – possibly even less. That's pretty much the marketing lifecycle of a new book release: six weeks to one month prior to the book coming out, the month of release itself, and (if you're fortunate) the month after. Once that time has passed, they'll move on to publicizing the next writer's book project, while yours disappears in the rear-view mirror.

Three months. That's roughly how long your book has to make a splash and generate some traction: just three months.

It's not impossible to create a little publicity after that three-month window is closed, but the likelihood is that you're going to have to out in most of the effort yourself.

The moral of this particular story is to make hay while the sun shines, as the old saying goes, because the lifespan of your book in marketing terms can often be very short indeed.

That's simply the nature of the publishing business. No matter how successful an author you are, today's hot new release is just waiting to become tomorrow's bargain bin deal. Books are a commodity, and just like any other commodity, they have a built-in shelf life. When all's said and done, it's best not to become too emotionally attached to them.

Rights

While having creative control is important to writers, the issue of ownership and rights is even more critical.

To the uninitiated, a book is simply that: a book, something that an author writes and then sells to a publisher or to the reader via a publisher/distributor. In reality, things are a little more complicated than that. Your intellectual property comes with all sorts of exciting potential: a book can be translated into many different languages and published in multiple countries, for example; recorded by a narrator and turned into an audiobook; even adapted for comic books, television, or the silver screen.

All of these facets — and several more besides — come in the form of *rights*. As the copyright owner, you get to license those rights to anybody who wants them, assuming that they're willing to pay for the privilege.

My self-published book *Haunted Healthcare*, for example, has been made available in English-language digital and print versions via Amazon KDP. It has also been released as an audiobook via the medium of ACX (the Audiobook Creation Exchange) and at the time of writing, I'm in talks with a major European publisher about the possibility of a Polish language version.

The more popular your book is, the more avenues of potential readership will open up. Unfortunately for you, the author, if you have chosen the traditional publishing route, a significant chunk of those intellectual property rights will have been signed over to the publishing house. Sometimes it's a 50/50 split, but it's just as likely that the publisher will want to own one hundred percent of the rights in perpetuity — in other words, you're signing those rights away.

Forever.

Imagine, if you will, that your book takes off. I mean, *really* takes off. Think Andy Weir with *The Martian*. You've written a bestselling novel or nonfiction book. The publisher now has you over a barrel, because they'll be raking in the money from every one of those ancillary rights that they are able to farm out to prospective purchasers. You'll see only a fraction of the proceeds from those deals yourself, because you didn't retain the subsidiary rights.

In effect, you're locked into a deal with the publisher, and you no longer own your own creation.

They do.

Think carefully before giving that up, lock, stock, and barrel.

Summing Up

Having come this far, it may seem that I'm pretty down on the world of traditional publishing. That really isn't the case. I have been blessed to get to work with some fine people, most of whom do their very best to make my trad books sell as well as they possibly can.

The traditional approach holds a number of great benefits,

particularly in the very early stages of an author's career, when placing a book with a reputable publisher can earn them a healthy amount of credibility and prestige.

Managing to get your book accepted by a publishing house is no small achievement, and signifies that the quality of your writing has reached a truly professional standard. That knowledge alone should instill a justifiable sense of satisfaction and pride in the fledgling writer.

At the risk of repeating myself once more, if one of your primary writing goals is to walk into a book store and see a book with your name on it sitting on the shelf, then this is the path for you. It's not one that you have to walk forever, or even exclusively, if you don't wish to.

Now let's take a look at a different road, and see whether it's a better path for you.

CHAPTER THIRTEEN

Self (Indie) Publishing

Pros

This method provides you with the greatest amount of control and flexibility during the writing and publishing process. You, the writer, are responsible for every single aspect of the book's production: the writing, formatting, editing, cover design, sales, marketing, you name it...it's your responsibility to make it happen.

Needless to say, having such a huge amount of creative freedom comes with quite a considerable downside: you have to put in a phenomenal amount of hard work in order to get everything done. That usually comes down to you either a) doing it yourself, or b) subcontracting the job out, and paying somebody else to do it for you.

We've already talked about many of the positive aspects to choosing this particular route on your journey toward publication. I won't belabor the point, but let's recap some of them here:

You set the price, which means that you can vary it as and when you choose — which in turn means that you can set up promotional flash sales, offering the book at a discount for a certain period of time, in order to attract more readers. This is an extremely useful option for those writers who release multiple books in a series. For example, on the same day that the latest book in that particular series is published, the writer drops the price of the first book to something a little more attractive…let's say a dollar or two, at most. This can have the effect of drawing in new readers by attracting them with the discounted price on book one, and then pointing them toward the new release just at it hits the market.

You get to create your own advertising campaigns and tailor them to suit your needs (and budget). There are a lot of options out there for the self-published writer to publicize his or her work. Bookbub and Amazon advertisements are just two of the better-known options. While a traditional publisher may have stopped pushing your book two months or so after its release, you have the option to keep promoting it through these channels for as long as it suits you to do so. The only person who can give up on your book is *you*.

Nothing kills the chances of a book doing well more effectively than a bad cover. *Nothing*. As previously mentioned, a couple of my trad covers have been somewhat less than successful. Fortunately for me, I was able to connect with a graphic designer whose work is nothing short of amazing. This guy turns out high-quality covers in just a day or two, and charges a very reasonable fee to do so. Stellar work that's very affordable, and delivered promptly? He's a dream come true, and it makes all the difference when it comes down to making book sales.

This commonality of cover design also helps to keep all of my books consistently on-theme, something that will be discussed when we talk about branding in the next chapter.

Trad publishers can't match the royalty share being offered by publishers like Amazon, with their 35%—70% rates making the 7-25% rates pale by comparison. On a per-book basis, indie publishing currently has no equal.

Another benefit if that author copies are usually cheaper when you put out your own work, costing somewhere between $3.50 and $6 on average, versus the $8—$12 of traditional publishers. Generally speaking, the smaller the publishing house, the more expensive their author copies. It's not that they're trying to rip off their writers; larger companies such as Amazon are able to leverage greater economies of scale, and can therefore afford to sell you copies of your book for significantly less money per unit than the little guys can.

This sometimes manifests itself in a rather strange way. Every once in a while, it's a good idea to browse online retailer sites to see how your book is charting. I was surprised to see paperback copies of one of my books selling for just $7 and change on Amazon. The publisher was charging me more than that ($9.21, to be precise) for author copies, so I purchased as many copies of the book as the retailer would allow me to buy and refreshed my stock of inventory with it — you should always keep 5-10 copies of your book on hand for direct sale at talks, conventions, and other similar events.

The following week, the book was still priced at $7 so, knowing a bargain when I saw one, I bought ten more copies. Then I wrote to the head of the publishing house, not in an attempt to be rude, but to make him aware of a situation that was financially hurting not only his authors, but also his own sales of author copies. Although supporting your publishing house is the right and proper thing to do, the profit margins on book sales are relatively slim, even when the writer sells them directly to the reader. It makes no sense for the writer to pay more for author copies than it costs to purchase retail copies; none whatsoever. We are literally giving money away.

In addition to that, there's the fact that buying books from the online retailer kicks in a couple of extra benefits for the author. Firstly, I gained a royalty payment (albeit small) on each purchase, which put a little of my own money back into my pocket; and secondly, each sale increased the book's position in the chart rankings for its particular category, boosting its visibility and putting it in front of more potential readers.

Whichever way I looked at it, buying discounted retail copies was a win/win proposition for me. The head of the publishing house, which had changed ownership since I first wrote the book for them, wrote back to me and said that he had instructed his sales department to offer me a 60% discount on future author copies of my book.

Publishing is a business, and therefore it's wise to keep personal emotions out of it, but it was hard for me to not feel as if I'd been taken advantage of by the publisher up to that point. They could have offered me a 60% discount all along, and still made themselves a healthy profit on all of the author copies I had bought before then, which numbered in the hundreds. It was only when I'd pointed out the disparity and said that I would buy from the retailer in future that they had offered me that discount.

So much for the publisher having loyalty to their stable of writers. The net effect of this exchange between the publisher and I was twofold. To this day, I still buy copies of the book from Amazon instead of from them; it also had the effect of pushing me even more firmly in the direction of indie publishing.

Subsidiary Rights

Lastly but by no means least, we return to the issue of subsidiary rights. When you sell your book to a publisher, you're selling not only the book itself, but also an entire universe of potential. Audio, international/foreign language, and TV rights are gone when you sign that contract. Some publishers will leave you with 50% of those rights, but many want to keep them all for themselves, on the off-chance that you happened to write the next *Da Vinci Code*.

Those intellectual property rights may not seem like much when you're first starting out, but if you mean to keep on writing, then they could be a very big deal just a few years down the line. Self-publishing lets you retain control over the many various forms and markets in which your work can be sold and distributed.

A couple of years ago, I received a Facebook message from a reader which contained a link to an Amazon product page.

"I can't wait to read this book!" the reader enthused. "Can I get a signed copy when it comes out?"

Now that's odd, I thought, clicking on the link and finding the release date for the book in question. *I don't have any books coming out that month...*

But that was my name on the appropriately spooky cover, and the book seemed like exactly the sort of thing I would write. With a frown, I looked up the product details. The publisher wasn't one that I had ever contracted with, but the sales copy (the small chunk of text that the publisher uses to try and hook a potential reader) sounded a lot like one of my other titles.

Confused, I contacted my publisher for clarification. They were able to clear up the mystery straight away. Without letting me know, they had sold the subsidiary rights for my book to another publisher, one who specialized in putting out library editions of more adult books, edited down and aimed at younger readers.

"Do I still get paid royalties for this?" I asked, not wanting to feel as if my work had been Shanghaied. As things turned out, I *did* get paid a small amount for each copy sold, but what bothered me was the fact that this had all been done without my knowledge. I had no real right to complain; when I had signed the contract with the publisher, I had signed over all of the ancillary rights to my manuscript. The publishing house was perfectly within their rights to do what they did, and a friend made the point that how often in life do you get paid for work that you never actually did in the first place?

That was my first encounter with the murky waters of subsidiary rights. In the grand scheme of things, I didn't really lose anything — in fact, I made a handful of dollars on the library book deal — but I was somewhat taken by surprise at just how easily my words could be repackaged, repurposed, and sold on without any input from me whatsoever.

When it comes to the realm of indie publishing, on the other hand, this would never have happened. Two years ago, a European publisher contacted me with an enquiry about translating one of my books into German. We negotiated a fair and equitable deal directly. The book duly saw print, with a completely different cover (I had no input on this, but rather liked the finished product) and it still sells moderately well in that market. Each year, I receive an agreed-upon royalty payment from the German publisher. This is how I intend to handle all future subsidiary rights negotiations, except for the unlikely event that Hollywood comes calling — in that case, I'll bite the bullet and seek out an agent that specializes in brokering movie deals.

Who knows, maybe one day that will be more than a pipe dream...

Cons

You have complete control. Over *everything*.

Well, practically everything. With the exception of a few limited constraints that will be imposed upon you by Amazon, Draft2Digital, Smashwords, or whatever else you choose to be your platform, the responsibility for the final product lies with you.

If the book is a success, the lion's share of the credit goes to you.

If the book is a failure, then it's your fault. Completely. One hundred percent.

Remember that old saying about success having a

multitude of fathers, but failure only having one? That would be you — a failed book is going to be totally and utterly *your* fault.

Sound daunting? It can be, but it doesn't have to be. I'm not trying to scare or discourage you, but at the same time, I would be remiss if I didn't give you a reality check here. The good news is that all of the tools you need to produce a top notch book are out there, and with a little hard work — plus, it must be pointed out, a small investment of money, which should pay you great dividends in the long run — it is possible for the final product to look every bit as professional as something a major publishing house would put out.

Writing is, for the most part, fun. Proofing, editing, marketing, and sales chores are generally not. The business aspects of publishing are, to put it bluntly, a real pain in the arse, but you must learn to master them if you want to put your words in front of as many readers as possible. (That *is* the ultimate goal, right?)

As an indie writer, your book probably won't end up in any of the bigger chain bookstores, but seeing it on the shelves of your local mom and pop book shop isn't a complete impossibility — though it may require a little leg work on your part.

And that, my friends, is it — my cons list for self-publishing. There are lots of benefits to be reaped, and very few drawbacks…*if* you're willing to put in a little hard work.

CHAPTER FOURTEEN

The Hybrid Author

This, in case you haven't already figured it out, is my preferred option. By far.

I wouldn't recommend it for the casual writer, but if you have your heart set on a career — actually building yourself 'the write life,' as I like to call it — then this is, I'm convinced, the way to go. It allows you to leverage the best of both worlds, marrying up the trad and indie sides of the table into (you guessed it) a hybrid of both.

As a working writer who's in it for the long haul, I firmly believe that this is the best way to have your cake and eat it too.

The career path I recommend goes something like this: Whether or not you start by self-publishing your first book, fairly early on in your writing career, you should begin to court traditional publishers, sending out query letters and proposals to those who seem like a good fit for you.

Once you beat the slush pile and get your first published book out there, you'll experience the satisfaction of seeing your book on display at a brick and mortar book store. You can now use this as your calling card when you submit proposals to other publishing houses (or the same one that initially published you) as you have established a degree of credibility by demonstrating that your writing is of a publishable standard. You have been judged and found to be capable by one of the gatekeepers of traditional publishing, and that counts for a lot. If you decide to venture into the world of trad publishing once more, you'll find it a lot easier to gain acceptance the second time around.

After having one or more books released by a publishing house, it's now a good time to diversify into the world of self-publishing. You use your trad book(s) as a springboard; buyers are often more confident in the value of a product if it's traditionally published, especially if they've been burned by buying something self-published in the past, only to find it to be of questionable quality. If you can hook them with your trad work, then they're much more likely to try some of your self-published fare afterward, once they've decided that they like your writing style. Numerous readers have written to tell me that this is how they first got into my books.

And that is pretty much that. Wash, rinse, and repeat — or, as those paragons of self-publishing, Sterling and Stone, put it in their superb book of the same title: *Write. Publish.*

Repeat. (If you haven't read it, I can't recommend that particular book highly enough).

Now, let's break down the two major paths — traditional and self-publishing — a little bit further. The techniques that I am about to lay out for you have worked well for me as I have built my own writing life. None of them are secret, or particularly clever in nature. While there are no guarantees when it comes down to getting published, these roadmaps will, I believe, offer you a solid plan for success. They are by no means the *only* way to achieve your goal, but they have been proven to work, and can help to guide you along your own path to publication.

CHAPTER FIFTEEN

Road Map: Traditional Publishing

Becoming a published author is a journey, so it only seems appropriate that yours should begin with an actual, physical journey — in this case, to the nearest bookstore. Once there, head straight to the section that covers the type of book that you're planning to write. Most of the books should be shelved sideways-on, with their spines facing outward. Pay close attention to the logos imprinted on those spines, because you're looking for the ones that appear in the greatest numbers. Now, note down the names of the most successful publishers, or those whose titles best fit your book's theme. Make a list of them all.

I went to Barnes and Noble, Boulder's biggest bookstore, and made a bee-line for the metaphysical/mystical section. There was a wide range of books, covering subjects as diverse as ghosts/hauntings, UFOs, Bigfoot/cryptids, Tarot, conspiracy theories, and other similar 'new age' subjects.

One logo that really stood out was that of a publisher whose books appeared over and over again as I scanned across the titles on each shelf.

I knew that I'd be writing a book set in the paranormal non-fiction genre. The more of their books that I saw and quickly studied, the more I thought they would be a great fit for me. After leaving the store and heading home, I went online to check out their web page, with the intention of learning a little more about them.

They'd been in business since 1901, and were now the world's largest publisher in the field of mind, body, and spirit (which includes the paranormal). Their vision statement proudly declared that their goal was "to be the world's leading provider of works for personal growth, and the transformation of body, mind and spirit."

Now *that* sounded like somebody I wanted to partner with.

The next step can be taken care of from the comfort of your own home. Browse Amazon.com for titles similar to the sort of book you intend to write. For example, if your heart is set on writing a vampire novel, *Salem's Lot* by Stephen King and *Dracula* by Bram Stoker are both excellent starting points (not to mention damn fine reads in their own right).

At the time of writing this book, *Salem's Lot,* published by Random House, is at #4 in the *Vampire Horror* category. At

#3 is *The Savage Earth*, book one of the *Vampire World Saga*, by P.T. Hylton and Jonathan Benecke. This title, the first in a six-book series, is published by First Light Books. Good old Dr. Google doesn't show any web pages for a publisher by this name, which suggests that the book may well be self-published. It has a great cover and nearly 150 reviews, with a 4.5-star average rating. Other books in this same series also appear at positions #9, #10, #11, and #13 in the same category. Hats off to Messrs. Hylton and Benecke for owning a huge chunk of real estate in the *Vampire Horror* sub-genre on Amazon.

Coming in at #2 is the classic Anne Rice novel *Interview with the Vampire*, also published by Random House. Finally, in an unexpected turn of events, the #1 spot is occupied by *Hot Werewolf MC: A Paranormal Romance Series Box Set*, by Abby Apple. This title is an omnibus edition that collects four novels about, and I'm quoting here, "hot werewolf bikers." Although not vampire-centric, this self-published supernatural/romance genre mashup is doing well enough to beat out the master himself, Stephen King, and also holds the top spot in the *American Horror* category. 901 pages of fiction for less than $0.99 (or free, for members of Kindle Unlimited) seems to be attracting a lot of readers, and more power to Ms. Apple for marketing her book so effectively.

What have we learned so far? That, of the top four titles in *Vampire Horror*, two are self-published, and two are traditionally published by one of the big, well-established houses.

Look at the top-selling books in your category. Who has published them? Make a list of the top five. Then go to each publisher's website and see which ones have open submission policies. Highlight those.

Sticking with the *Vampire Horror* theme, Random House does not have an open submissions policy. Their website states:

Penguin Random House LLC does not accept unsolicited submissions, proposals, manuscripts, or submission queries via email at this time. If you would like to have your work or manuscript considered for publication by a major book publisher, we recommend that you work with an established literary agent.

So, there you have it; and frankly, it's no big surprise. Landing a book deal with Random House is the equivalent of an indie film-maker getting her foot in the door at Paramount Pictures. The odds of it happening first time out are nothing short of astronomical. Better to set one's sights a little lower on the food chain (or, as the web site advises, attempt to get a literary agent interested in their manuscript)…either that, or consider the possibility a traditional publisher may not be the best place for their vampire horror novel to find a home, and think about publishing it themselves.

I did the exact same thing with the *Ghosts and Hauntings* category back when I was trying to find a publisher. Browsing that same category today, I'm happy to see my own books occupying positions #8, #12, #20, and #23.

All four of those books are self-published.

Coming in at #56, however, is my first love — *In Search of the Paranormal*, which was published traditionally. A quick check of their website reveals that they have an open submission policy. So do the publishers of the book in the #1 position: *The World's Most Haunted House*, by William J. Hall.

Let's take a look at those guidelines, shall we? (You can find the full document at *https://www.llewellyn.com/about/author_submissions.php*)

"Listen carefully to your patient," a wise old doctor once said to his student. "Because the patient is trying to tell you what's wrong." The same is true with submissions guidelines. A publisher's time is valuable. They have none to waste. They therefore like to tell prospective writers up-front, exactly what kind of pitch, proposal, or manuscript will satisfy their requirements.

We accept submissions directly from authors (including first time authors) and from literary agents.

Our emphasis is on the practical. how it works, how it is done, and self-help material. best-selling subject areas include:
  Alternative health
  Astral projection/BE
  [long list of topics...snip]
  Yoga

The list, which runs to some 28 discrete topics, provides a lot of scope for potential authors. With that being said, if your book doesn't fall into one of those areas, it's probably not worth pitching to this publisher. While there's always an outside chance that they might love your idea *so* much that they are willing to go beyond their own rules, it's extremely unlikely; the odds are that you'll just waste their time, and yours. Far better to go in search of a different publisher, one whose catalog aligns more closely with the type of book you are passionate about writing.

By listing those 28 areas, the publisher is basically telling you which category your book needs to fall under if they're going to consider it for publication. *Listen to them*. It's amazing how many would-be authors don't, choosing to believe instead that their idea is *so* good, the rules don't actually apply to them.

They're almost always mistaken.

Please note: we do not publish poetry books, children's books, spiritual or new age fiction, channeled books, cook books, or picture books.

Once again, they're telling you how not to waste their time, or yours.

Original manuscripts are preferred. We do not reproduce previously published or self-published works.

Most publishers take a similar stance. Unless it's something truly remarkable, such as the cultural phenomenon that was

Andy Weir's *The Martian* (originally published for free on the Internet) they're not interested in retreading old ground. Don't try to repackage and repurpose something you've already put out there in some other form.

Query letters, manuscripts, and proposals may be sent via email to: submissions@publishersname.com

Word documents sent as one file in an email attachment are preferred. please be sure to number the pages.

I once spoke with a literary agent who complained about the number of submissions she received in which the would-be author simply cut and pasted their proposal directly into the body of the email. In order for your proposal to be taken seriously, it should be formatted nicely and look neat on the printed page. Can you imagine the end result of printing out a 10,000-word proposal directly from an email client? The poor agent or acquisitions editor's eyes would be bleeding by the end of it.

Even at this early stage, they are going to be looking at your use of line spacing, punctuation, and paragraphs. This is your first opportunity to impress them with the neatness of your layout.

In the same vein, you need to be scrupulous about finding typos and spelling mistakes. The more professional your initial presentation is from the outset, the more likely it is that the publisher will want to work with you. Acquisitions editors and their colleagues are usually deluged with poorly written, badly executed book proposals. Don't let yours be one of them. It's important to remember that nobody actually *wants* to waste their time. An open submission window means that the publishing house would like nothing more than to see a stream of well thought out, finely crafted project proposals hitting their inbox.

Now, we get to the real meat and potatoes. As such, I'll break it down point by point, and include elements of my own successful pitch to give you an idea of what the publisher may be looking for (remember, there are no guarantees):

Your submission *must* include the following:

Note the use of the word **must.** These are not 'guidelines,' despite the name. Treat them as ironclad requirements.

Cover letter containing a brief description of the project and the contents of the package.

The cover letter is a job interview. It should offer up a quick elevator pitch (your opportunity to sell the concept behind your book in a few brief paragraphs) and establish your credentials as an author, while also giving a smattering of information about your own personal background. Here's my cover letter for a book that would, in a slightly different form, be accepted by a publishing house.

For the attention of: Acquisitions Editor <name redacted>
Richard Estep
Friday, January 17th, 2014
My Street Address
My Town
My State
My Zip Code

Dear <acquisitions editor>,

A cloaked spectral figure pursues me across a misty graveyard at night; an encounter with satanic forces in a desolate cornfield; and an inhuman scream emanating from thin air inside a derelict English church; these are just three otherworldly encounters detailed in my book Fear in the Night: Two Decades Spent Hunting Ghosts. The book contains a selection of my creepiest and most intense investigations, culled from a casebook begun in 1995, and covering cases in both the United Kingdom and the United States. Per our recent discussion, I would respectfully like to submit my manuscript for your consideration.

Presently I am a volunteer firefighter-paramedic in the county of Boulder, Colorado. I work as a clinical educator for a national ambulance corporation; teach medicine to students at several paramedic training academies; and serve on a federal disaster medical response team. In addition to my emergency response career, I am the founder and director of the Boulder County Paranormal Research Society, which actively investigates cases of haunting and other paranormal claims throughout the State of Colorado and surrounding environs. Being a transplanted Brit, I have spent the past eighteen years investigating haunted houses on two continents. I also hold an AA degree in Paramedicine.

Although I have never been published before, I have lectured extensively in the fields of paranormal investigation and emergency response. Most recently, I interwove the two subjects for a series of lectures at the DragonCon convention in Atlanta, where I was a guest speaker. I also appeared in the 2008 documentary film The Ghosts of Elitch Theatre. *Additionally, the website about.com featured me as a presenter for several of their paranormal video segments in 2012.*

Thank you for reading my manuscript. Please feel free to contact me at any time via email or cell: (123) 456 7891. I look forward to hearing from you.

Sincerely,
Richard Estep

The first paragraph is the hook, hopefully your way of getting the reader interested in the project, if only in a very preliminary way. The second and third, which with hindsight, I believe are a little too wordy, demonstrate that I have some sort of professional background. Finally, we close with some direct contact information and some basic courtesy.

No cover letter should *ever* be more than a single page in length. Remember that the reader, no matter if it's an editor or an intern, will be put off by any grammatical errors, typos, or sloppy formatting. The cover letter is usually their first exposure to you, and taking the time to get it right is similar to wearing smart attire when you go to a job interview. It speaks volumes about your professionalism.

Make sure that your first impression isn't also your last impression.

An outline and/or annotated table of contents

Before moving forward on a project, publishers like to make sure that, rather than some half-baked idea, what they are buying into is going to have a beginning, a middle, an end, and some kind of coherent structure. This harkens back to the outline you drew up during the planning phase of your manuscript, and in fact can be lifted directly from that document (you *did* keep a copy of it, right?)

This is the original outline for *Fear in the Dark*. When compared with the book that ultimately saw print, it actually matches the final manuscript very closely (though there are one or two differences). I used this outline as the framework for each chapter of the book, and it turned out to be well worth the time I invested in planning it out. It made the actual writing process go by very smoothly, and cured me of ever wanting to be a pantser again.

More to the point, though, it was letting the publisher know what the book would finally look like. It proved that I had a vision for the project (one which they reserved the right to modify, but wouldn't significantly change) which had a fighting chance to be turned into reality.

Fear in the Night: Two Decades Spent Hunting Ghosts
Outline/table of contents

Introduction
- A death in the family
- My first dead body
- Shell-shocked
- A sideways step

Chapter 1 – Reality Check
- A Little About Me

- Reality Check
- A Dead Baby in our Bathtub?
- The Team

Chapter 2 – A Ghostly Road
- Growing Up Ghostly
- Haunted Hull
- The Old Lady
- Two Apparitions
- School Spirits
- A Poltergeist Named Arthur
- The Keith Richards of the Paranormal
- Return to the Demon Church

Chapter 3 – The Beast in the Tower
- "This Place Changes After Dark"
- Animal Sacrifice
- Ritual Desecration
- The Beast
- A Lesson Learned
- Borley Rectory
- We Are Not Alone

Chapter 4 – Who's Out There?

☐ A Lonely Place to Be

☐ A Light in the Darkness

☐ Drunk, Not Demonic

☐ Bluffing

☐ Secret Security

☐ Be Careful What You Wish For

Chapter 5 – Horror Comes Calling

☐ Lights in the Tower

☐ Don't Turn Around

☐ Footsteps Amongst the Graves

☐ Malicious Breathing

☐ The Screech

☐ The Most Terrifying Sight…

Chapter 6 - Aftermath

☐ Results

☐ Locals Clash with Satanists

☐ Still Active

Chapter 7 – Private Case: Conjuring Evil

☐ A Single Mother

- Dark Magic
- Overnight Lockdown
- Light and Noise
- Who's Crying?

Chapter 8 – Theatrical Spirits
- Welcome to the Theater
- Ghost Light
- Holding Vigil
- Doorway to Darkness

Chapter 9 – Lady Jane's Ghost
- Queen for Nine Days
- Beheaded
- A Ghostly Coach and Horses
- Staking Out the Ruins
- Flare up

Chapter 10 – Haunted London
- The Bloody Tower
- Procession of the Dead
- Executed Royalty Returns
- "I'm Playing with Those Two Boys, Daddy"

- Murder at The Grenadier
- Money for His Soul
- Down in the Cellar

Chapter 11 – Atlantic Crossing
- Relocating
- 9/11
- Goodbye from Beyond?

Chapter 12 – The Hammer House Murder
- A Brutal Murder
- Tired, Shivering, and Anxious
- Seeing it Through
- "This House is Clean!"

Chapter 13 – The Firemen Who Could Not Rest
- Morticians and Masons
- A Tragic Accident
- The Hand at the Window
- The Car That Drove Itself
- Who Started the Engine?
- A Hotbed of EMF
- Heavy Breathing

☐ Call the Psychic
☐ Next Stop: Denver Fire

Chapter 14 – Carl's Ghost
☐ The Face at the Window
☐ A Winter's Night
☐ Feeling Uneasy
☐ "Carl, Can You Hear Us?"
☐ The Camera's Dead
☐ Shadow Figure
☐ "Terrible, Disturbing Dreams"
☐ Threats in the Mail

Chapter 15 – Private Case: Haunted House of Angels
☐ A House Full of Angels
☐ Molested
☐ Muffled Voices
☐ It Wants to Come In
☐ A Dark and Hooded Figure
☐ Overnight
☐ The Real Enemy

Chapter 16 – Historic Hotel Haunting

- ☐ Years of Sightings
- ☐ Suicide Pact
- ☐ The Woman in White
- ☐ 302 and 304
- ☐ "Careful!"
- ☐ "I'll Never Go Back!"

A description of the intended market as it pertains to the subject matter, including an explanation of why someone would want to buy the book.

"Just who, exactly, is the target audience for this book?" It's a fair question, isn't it? If you're trying to write the definitive history of early Hungarian cabinet-making, then you are, by definition, restricting yourself to a fairly small, niche market of readers: early Hungarian cabinet-making enthusiasts. That's a book which either a) probably won't see print, or b) will find a welcome home, but only at a *very* specialized publishing house.

   This question is answered by market research, pure and simple. If you have followed my advice thus far, you will already have done much of the legwork required before ever typing the first word of your manuscript. This came in the form of hunting through the various Amazon categories and subcategories to find a match for the type of book you wanted to write.

With the book description for *Fear in the Night*, my intent was to paint a picture of a diverse, colorful book that would appeal to several different types of reader.

Here's the description of the intended market:

Fear in the Night spans nearly two decades of nights spent in haunted houses. The first half of the book covers my British cases, and the second half relates those from the United States. I have chosen the most chilling, interesting, and sometimes just plain weird cases from my journals.

This book is ideal reading material for the person who loves a true ghost story – which most people do. Locations range from the Tower of London to a former orphanage in Colorado. The historic nature of some locations (such as an old firehouse or a pub which used to be frequented by the Duke of Wellington) will also appeal to history buffs. I have endeavored to include something for everyone, and to give the book a broad appeal.

Include a list of known competing titles and how yours

differs.

At the risk of disagreeing with a publisher, I choose not to see similar books to mine as being direct competition. In fact, I believe the opposite to be true. Just like most writers, I am a voracious reader — that's exactly why I wanted to became a writer in the first place. The fact that you're reading this book makes me believe that you are probably much the same.

Let's say I discover a book that I really like from an author that is completely new to me. We'll use one of my favorite writers, Sir Terry Pratchett, as an example. His Discworld books have given me countless hours of enjoyment down through the years.

Pratchett co-authored a book with Neil Gaiman, the laugh-out-loud funny *Good Omens*. It's one of those novels where the sum of the whole is far greater than the individual parts. After reading that, I went on to seek out more books by Gaiman, and still make a point of doing so to this day. (Sadly, Sir Terry has since left us, but I've read everything he's ever published).

It isn't an either/or situation. Buying a Pratchett novel wouldn't prevent me from picking up a Gaiman, and vice versa. In fact, quite the opposite was true. I'd eagerly devour both, and when I was done, seek out something by yet another author whose style was similar to theirs.

This isn't a zero sum game. In other words, one author doesn't have to lose in order for another to win. We can *all* win.

Take, for example, my book *Haunted Healthcare.* It's one of my more popular titles. According to its listing page on Amazon.com, *Haunted Healthcare* is frequently bought alongside copies of *Supposedly Haunted: True Life Experiences of a Paranormal Investigator,* by E.E. Bensen, and *Cops' True Stories of the Paranormal: Ghosts, UFOs and Other Shivers,* by Loren W. Christensen. Now, I've never met Loren W. Christensen before, but E.E. Bensen happens to be a good friend of mine. In addition to investigating many locations together, he and I co-authored a book, *A Haunting at Farrar: Investigating One of the World's Most Haunted Schools.*

E.E. Bensen, Loren Christensen and I, all share an audience. We write similar books (paranormal non-fiction, with an emphasis on ghosts) and so it makes sense that we have a readership in common. I've read both of E.E. Bensen's books and greatly enjoyed them, and Loren's is on my future reading list. Our readers are doing much the same thing. I applaud when somebody buys a book by one of my peers, not least because there's a good chance that they'll find their way to my work someday too. Rooting for the success of your peers is also the decent thing to do.

In the eyes of a traditional publisher, other publishers are the competition. A dollar spent on a book released by a different publishing house is a book that could, they think, have been better spent on one of their own. A savvy self-published writer, on the other hand, sees the work of their peers as potential opportunity, rather than a threat.

My submission for *Fear in the Dark* contained the following list of 'competing titles:'

Adventures of a Ghost Hunter: My Investigations into the Darkness, by Adam Nori (Llewellyn, 2013)

Ghost Hunting: True Stories of Unexplained Phenomena from The Atlantic Paranormal Society, by Jason Hawes and Grant Wilson (Gallery Books, 2007)

Seeking Spirits: The Lost Cases of The Atlantic Paranormal Society, by Jason Hawes and Grant Wilson (Gallery Books, 2009)

Coast To Coast Ghosts: True Stories of Hauntings Across America, by Ann Rule (Andrews McMeel, 2001)

There are numerous similar titles currently on the market. Mine differs in the fact that it covers a broad spectrum of cases across two continents, blending the different flavors of British and American paranormal research into a compelling mix of the old world and the new.

In the case of a proposal, at least three sample chapters.

Note the use of the words *at least*. It tacitly invites the applicant to submit more, and that's exactly what I did, turning in five completed chapters and an introduction. This demonstrates a willingness to go above and beyond the minimum requirements, and, assuming that the work is of at least semi-publishable quality, it should also bolster the editor's confidence in the ability of the writer to complete the manuscript.

If you have already written the entire book, you can certainly submit the whole thing. Editors know what I taught you earlier in this book: that a completed manuscript can always be restructured or edited, but there's always a risk that an incomplete one will never see the light of day. At the very least, however, try to put four or five chapters into your submission, and make sure that they are your *best* chapters. There's no rule which states they must be chapters one through five, after all. If the strongest portion of your book is the middle, cherry pick from there.

Submissions must be in **English, double-spaced with 1-inch margins in 12-point type.**

You disobey this rule at your peril. In fact, failure to stick to these specifications *exactly* may result in your manuscript getting tossed out, no matter how good the writing is. Editors are very particular about the formatting of the manuscripts they read, which is why the language, spacing, and margin requirements are written in bold type. I'm frankly surprised they aren't also underlined.

Getting this wrong is one of the fastest and simplest ways to rejection. Don't let your chance at publication become a casualty of something this obvious.

Please **number the pages** *and include a table of contents.*

Again with the bold highlighting! Numbering the pages of your manuscript takes no time at all. There's no excuse for getting this wrong.

Complete permissions and citations.

Everybody mentioned in the book (under their real name, at least) needs to sign a standardized document, giving permission for their name to appear in print. If that's not possible, the names can be changed into aliases.

Permission forms must also be supplied for any photographs that will appear in your book, signed by the photographer and/or copyright holder (none are needed if you have taken them yourself). Most publishers have standard permission forms that are available for download from their website, or can be emailed to you by the editorial staff.

If you're quoting a person or a published work, those sources must be cited as references. Some excellent feedback came from the editor of one of my books, who pointed out that I used the phrase "*it is said that...*" a great deal, when it came down to some of the ghost stories associated with the locations I was investigating. After reviewing the manuscript with a critical eye, I realized that he was absolutely right. I had used that phrase no less than thirteen times. I went to my personal library of paranormal non-fiction and sourced as many of those references as possible, putting them into a written document for the publisher. Although that source document wasn't ultimately a part of the finished book on publication, it proved to the editor that I had indeed done my homework, and wasn't simply making it up as I went along.

Total/estimated word count (generally we look for 50,000+ words, depending upon the project).

The publisher is giving aspiring writers another opportunity to avoid a common pitfall here. Despite the use of the word *generally*, proposed projects should be longer than 50,000 words if they are to have the maximum chance of success — so if your manuscript isn't at least that long, you should either look for opportunities to extend it (without adding meaningless padding) or consider a different publishing house.

Estimated date of completion.

Your chances of success are significantly improved if the answer to this question is "now."

Use of epigraphs should only appear at the start of sections or chapters; length is preferably no longer than 2 lines. All other quoting requires citation and mid-chapter epigraphs are not allowed.

Epigraphs are, essentially, short quotes that add a little flavor to a book. Liberally sprinkled throughout, usually at the beginning of each chapter, for example, they act as a kind of garnish. Use too many, and you run the risk of breaking up the flow of the piece. Once again, obey the publisher's stipulation where they are concerned (I would suggest either opening each chapter with a short epigraph, or simply not using them at all) otherwise you increase the risk of the manuscript being rejected.

Although it might seem like a lot at first, the requirements laid down by this particular publishing house are not really all that restrictive or onerous. Meet them, and your manuscript will receive fair and serious consideration for possible publication. Fail to do so, and it will almost certainly be a case of 'thanks, but no thanks.' If you have gone to all the trouble of writing a book proposal and have your heart set on traditional publication, spending a few extra minutes (or even hours) dotting the Is and crossing the Ts is a worthwhile investment indeed.

A word on the subject of simultaneous submissions/pitches — this is almost always a bad idea. If you're unfamiliar with the concept, simultaneous submissions or pitches means sending your manuscript or book proposal to multiple different publishers at the same time.

You probably wouldn't dream of proposing marriage to more than one person at the same time, right? Well, submitting your ideas to multiple editors simultaneously is the publishing world's equivalent. Let's say you send your manuscript to publishers A and B. Publisher A receives it, recognizes that it meets the submissions guidelines that have been set forth, and after a cursory look, decides that she likes what she sees. She's going to set it aside and give it a more thorough review when she has time, which may not be for another month or so, given how busy she is.

Publisher B, on the other hand, sees your submission and *instantly* know that it's a perfect fit for his publishing house; in fact, it's exactly the sort of project he has been looking for. After taking a few days to scrutinize the manuscript, and finding that it needs nothing more than a few minor tweaks to render it publishable, emails you back to offer conditional acceptance of your manuscript.

This is wonderful news for everybody except publisher A, who, if she has mentioned your book as a potentially good prospect to her colleagues and bosses, now has egg on her face when she receives word from you that your book is no longer available for publication. Whatever time and effort she has already put in (remember, time is at a premium for professionals in any industry) is now wasted.

Without knowing it, you have just burned a bridge, one of the last things you ever want to do in the writing field. It's a relatively small pond. Agents and editors talk to one another all the time, both officially and unofficially. You don't want to develop a reputation for reneging on your word when it comes to submitting work (or meeting deadlines, for that matter).

The right way to do it is also the most straightforward. Treat every submission like a rifle shot. Pick your target carefully, aiming for the publisher whose vision best aligns with yours. Craft a watertight proposal, and scrupulously comb it for errors until it is as letter-perfect as you can possibly make it. Then submit it to that one (and *only* that one) publisher.

And then...

...you wait.

I'm not going to lie. The waiting is the worst part. That, and the uncertainty. You've pulled the trigger. There is nothing more you can do but wait, and wait, and wait.

It's bloody interminable. The temptation is to keep checking your inbox every few hours, or even more often than that, if the anxiety starts to creep over you. You may very well lose sleep over it; at least, I did.

One thing that you must under no circumstances do, is to contact the publisher directly. You'll be tempted. *I'll just write or call to make sure that they received my submission*, says the voice in the back of your head. Don't give in to it. If you've heard nothing whatsoever after three months have passed, then sending a follow-up query is acceptable; nothing more than a brief, polite request for confirmation that the email or mailed package arrived as it should. But it's important to remember that a lot of publishing houses state openly that they will not get around to looking at unsolicited submissions for anywhere from six months to a year.

As tempting as it is, don't bug them. Precisely zero percent of the time, contacting the publisher to check on the status of your book will make that time pass faster. It may, on the other hand, piss off the editor, and no good can come of that.

At the risk of sounding negative, hope has no place in the publishing realm. Once the trigger has been pulled, events are almost completely out of your control. Although it's easier said than done, you need to put your submission completely out of your head. This means finding a coping mechanism (preferably a healthy one) and I have a specific one to suggest:

Start writing your next book.

No, I'm not kidding. You will have learned a number of lessons during the process of writing your first completed manuscript. Applying them to the business of writing book two means that it should be better than the first one, and therefore more likely to be successful.

The minute you hit the *send* button, take the rest of the day off. Find some way to reward yourself for achieving something that 99% of the people on this planet will never be able to say they have done: finished writing a book.

Go to the movies. Take your significant other out for dinner, because they've earned it (chances are, you've been a grouchy son of a bitch during this whole thing). Hang out with your friends for the night and rediscover what it means to have a social life. Whatever will help you to decompress, do that.

Then, the next day, sit your arse back down at your writing desk and start working on book two.

Dealing with Rejection

Despite your very best efforts, it's likely that your first attempt is going to result in rejection. At the risk of sounding harsh, get used to it. More rejection is coming.

If you're going to write professionally, or even just for fun, putting your work in front of other people is going to mean criticism and rejection. A writer needs to develop a very tough skin. The key thing is not to equate rejection of your work with rejection of you as a human being.

You are not your writing. It is a facet of you, yes, your creative self, manifesting through the medium of words, but there are plenty of excellent writers out there who are shitty human beings, and lots of wonderful people who cannot write proficiently. Writing ability, or the lack thereof, does not equate to your worth and value as a human being. Your Resistance-driven ego will try and convince you otherwise. Shout it down and drown it out.

Writing is a skill: no more, no less. Although we sometimes like to pretend that there's a sort of mystical muse, which comes down from on high when inspiration strikes, the truth is that stringing together words into sentences, paragraphs, and pages, is an acquired ability, no different than cooking, painting, or knitting. If you have some degree of natural talent, that will certainly help matters, but there is no substitute for perseverance and sheer hard work.

Pouring all of your hope, fear, anxiety, and nervous energy concerning the status of your pending submission into a second book will give you a *lot* of energy to harness. If rejection finally comes, then you may well be halfway to another project for submission — this one hopefully a little better — when it drops in to spoil your inbox like a turd in a punchbowl.

Rejections are *not* always absolute, so scrutinize them carefully. The proposal you have just read for *Fear in the Dark* was actually a follow-up to a rejection letter. I had originally proposed a book for wannabe paranormal investigators, teaching them some tips, tricks, and techniques. The acquisitions editor sent me a very polite rejection, but rather than dismissing my proposal out of hand, she was kind enough to give me a reason why: it wasn't the quality of my writing, but rather, the fact that in her opinion, most people learned how to ghost hunt from TV shows, not books. There were already a number of how to ghost hunt books on the market, and they just weren't selling well.

This was absolute gold as far as I was concerned. It left the door open for a follow-up inquiry, and I jumped on it, thanking the editor most sincerely for taking the time to explain her reasons for rejecting my work. What type of paranormal books, I asked, *were* selling these days?

I had no right to expect that she would answer me, but lo and behold, she did. Books containing real-life ghost stories were selling rather well, she explained, before asking whether I had anything along those lines.

I didn't, but after a frenzied night of writing, fueled by Monster energy drinks and six cups of tea, I had a complete book outline, five workable chapters, and a pitch ready to go. I sent it in the next day. That was the pitch for *Fear in the Dark* which appeared earlier in this chapter.

It's important to ask yourself whether you received a total rejection or a somewhat ambiguous, possibly even encouraging one? Consider any criticism you receive with great care.

I'm a huge fan of the *Warhammer* game (a range of fantasy and science fiction-themed tabletop miniatures made by Games Workshop). There's a vibrant universe of fiction based around the game, all run through Games Workshop's publishing house, Black Library. Once every year or two, Black Library opens up a submissions window, inviting members of the public to try their hand at writing a story based upon one of the Warhammer worlds.

I was excited at the prospect of branching out into fiction, especially in connection with an IP (intellectual property) that I had so much love for. After reading the submissions guidelines carefully, I put together a proposal consisting of a 500-word writing sample — basically just a single scene. Then I hit *send*, and did my very best not to think about the tantalizing prospect of writing about a galaxy full of mighty Space Marines and 'evil' alien species.

Three days later, I received an email from the Black Library. My hand was trembling with excitement as I clicked the mouse button to open it up.

It wasn't a rejection.

They liked my writing, and wanted to see more.

They. Wanted. To. See. More.

I'm sure that my hollering could be heard down at the end of the street. I was fanboying pretty hard for the rest of the day, walking on air. Now I was just a few thousand words away from making the grade and joining the hallowed ranks of *Warhammer* writers...

...right?

The guidelines had offered up several acceptable types of theme, one of which happened to be a ghost story. When I read that, my eyes lit up. Now *that* was firmly within my wheelhouse! My story concerned a small unit of infantry soldiers, lost behind enemy lines and about to be wiped out by alien forces. There was a distinctly supernatural slant, as one of the soldiers would turn out to be the spirit of a dead comrade.

The email from Black Library instructed me to send in a second writing sample, one that was more fleshed out, and a full-length outline, along with some brief character bios. No problem whatsoever. I sat down immediately, wrote the whole thing over the course of a day — this was only a short story, after all, not a novella or full-length novel — and sent it back. Ignoring my own good advice, I wandered around in a haze of gleeful anticipation for the next few weeks.

I deflated like a punctured balloon when the rejection

email arrived. In a serious funk, I nevertheless wrote a polite, respectful message back, asking if the editor could possibly share with me the reason why my pitch had been kicked back.

They were kind enough to do so. The stories they wanted to publish, the editor explained, would be epic in scope, painted on a grand canvas. The story that I had pitched to them was relatively small in scale, focusing on a tightly-knit unit of soldiers and a few alien adversaries. I hadn't really considered the idea of a ghost story being epic in scale, but apparently that's what they had in mind.

After the initial sense of dejection had passed, I realized that this was excellent feedback, and perhaps even a form of encouragement. Nobody had said that my quality of writing was below par; if it had been, they would never have asked for an extended sample. I simply would have gotten rejected in the first cut. Instead, the structure of my story just wasn't right for them. That was something I could work with, concrete information, and the next time that window opened up for public submissions, I would learn from that and submit something bigger and grander — with more explosions.

The lesson here is that not all rejections are permanent,

one hundred percent no-goes. Some editors may be willing to provide feedback, if you ask nicely. If you can, rewrite or resubmit your work based on their feedback. If not, send a gracious thank-you letter and move on, submitting your work to the next publisher on the list you made during the preliminary research stage of your project.

Keep submitting and learning from the feedback given in each rejection you receive. Those pitches and manuscripts should be getting better and better with every passing iteration.

Above all else, *don't give up.*

Acceptance

Congratulations — your proposal or manuscript has been accepted. Now you're off to the races!

Now, one hundred percent of your focus needs to be on working with the editor in order to turn out a publishable manuscript. Listen to the requests they make after the vision meeting (or whatever they choose to call it) and rewrite to editorial order. If there are any changes you feel are truly egregious, do your best to negotiate with them, working to find a middle ground that both sides can live with.

Above all else, do *not* get precious — by which I mean, dig in your heels and adopt an "It's my way or the highway" approach. The publisher is still well within their rights to cancel your contract, and it's not unknown for them to do just that if a writer becomes a big enough pain in the ass along the way. Remember that where a publishing house is concerned, a first-time author is just a commodity — no more, no less, and a disposable one at that. That may sound harsh, but it's true nonetheless. If you start to turn out a few moneymaking books for them, then it will be a different story. Until that day comes (assuming that it ever does) you have little or nothing in the way of leverage.

Most publishers will allow you to give input on the cover design, back cover copy, and other factors, but the truth is that your voice will most likely not be listened to if the publisher chooses not to. You have to be okay with that. I know that I'm starting to sound like a broken record, but remember: once the contract is signed, most of your rights go right along with your signature.

On to the Next One

Now for some good news. The majority of the blood, sweat, and tears in traditional publishing takes place when you're trying to sell your first book. It gets exponentially easier from there on.

It took me months to sell my first published book, *In Search of the Paranormal*. The second, *Haunted Longmont*, took just three days.

Why the disparity? I was able to leverage the fact that a tenured and respected publishing house had seen fit to publish my work. That told the editors at the second publishing house I was able to turn out a book that was of sufficient quality to sit on a bookstore shelf.

I pitched them a proposal to write the haunted history of my adopted hometown: Longmont, Colorado. After some brief discussion about the technical details, such as the expected word length and number of photographs that were required, we had a contract in no time at all. It made the process of writing and selling *In Search of the Paranormal* feel as though it took an age to complete.

The more books you have in print, the easier it becomes to get publishers interested in the next one — to a point. One thing worth considering is the size of the advance that you receive. As a general rule, I prefer to take the smallest advance possible most of the time. There rationale behind this is that a book is usually considered to be a success by the publisher if it earns back its advance — in other words, it makes back the amount of money they paid you to write it up front, and a little more on top to cover their costs.

If your book earns out its advance, you start to get paid royalties — small, regular (usually every six months) payments based upon the number of copies sold. If your book is successful enough to stay in print and keep making you royalties, the publisher has made money on you, not lost it. They are therefore more likely to give you a contract for another book.

Most often, I take a $1,000 advance. Half is usually paid on signing of the contract, with the other half being sent on acceptance of the manuscript for publication (once the publisher has signed off on it and is ready to send it to press). $1,000 is real money, but not so much that my books don't have a decent chance of earning it back.

Two good friends of mine co-wrote a book that paid out a $9,000 advance, which it never made back. Ten years later, it remains their only book in print.

Some publishers don't pay an advance at all. In that case, you get nothing upfront, but do at least start making royalty payments six months or less after the book's release date.

Smaller publishing houses generally have a set amount for their advance payments. It's typically not worth trying to haggle with them. I always feel grateful for whatever I do get, reminding myself of Stephen King's comment about what makes for a talented writer.

Cash the check and pay a bill with it – or treat myself to something a little more fun!

CHAPTER SIXTEEN

Roadmap: Indie Publishing

Choosing Your Publisher

Your book is now written, complete, edited, and ready to be published. You don't have to impress an agent or a publisher. You're going to keep control and put this one out yourself.

Without a doubt, the most important question to ask is: which distribution platform am I going to go with? The only gatekeepers potentially barring your way are technical specifications — the actual nuts and bolts of file formatting, cover sizing, and so on.

Generally speaking, the choice comes down to distributing to multiple sales platforms at the same time, or restricting yourself to one — and for the majority of indie writers, that one is usually Amazon.

At first, this sounds like a no-brainer. Why would you choose to restrict your work to just one retailer, when you could also put it out via the Apple bookstore, Barnes and Noble Online, Kobo books, and others?

The simple answer is that exclusivity has some very tangible rewards...and more than its fair share of drawbacks.

Amazon's Kindle platform has become the focal point of self-publishing in the United States and in a number of other countries (mostly in the English-speaking world), but it does *not* have an impressive market share in every single part of the world. There are some countries in which Jeff Bezos's' juggernaut has barely made a dent in the book retail market.

In addition to being able to put your book out in front of millions of potential readers, Amazon's big lure is the Kindle Select program. The company offers a service to its customers known as Kindle Unlimited, in which the customer pays a flat, monthly fee, and in exchange, can read an unlimited number of the books whose authors have signed them up for Kindle Select.

Each time a reader reads a single page of a Kindle Select book after checking it out of the Kindle Unlimited Library, Amazon pays the author a tiny royalty. Yes, this really is a negligible amount, usually somewhere around $0.0045 per page, but when *thousands* of pages are being read, it soon adds up to something like real money. As things stand at the time of writing (summer 2019) when 1,000 pages of a Kindle Unlimited book are read, the author makes $4.75.

To put this into perspective, I typically make around $40-$60 per day from Kindle Select borrows and page reads. That's $40-$60 for doing absolutely nothing, other than having my self-published back catalog enrolled in the Kindle Select program.

What's the downside? (Because there's always a downside, right?) The answer is that in order to be eligible for that per-page royalty, your book has to be exclusive to this one publishing platform. You cannot offer it via any other retailers. You, the writer, are essentially married to Amazon, the publisher...on a per-book basis, at least.

It's not unusual on any given day for one of my books to sell one single copy, or even none whatsoever, but to make me $20 from Kindle borrows. That's a financial benefit I would not have if the book wasn't enrolled in the Kindle Select program. On the flip side, however, I have to wonder how many potential sales I am losing out on by not having the book available for sale via Apple, Barnes and Noble, Kobo, etc.

Please note that Kindle Digital Publishing (KDP) and Kindle Digital Publishing *Select* (KDPS) are easily mixed up. If you publish via KDP but DON'T enroll your book in KDPS, you are still publishing via Amazon, but you are *not* restricted from publishing your book with other retailers. Think of it as something like an open marriage, if that helps. It's only when you sign up for select that you a) start making money on Kindle Unlimited borrows, and b) are now locked into an exclusive detail with Amazon for the English language versions of your books.

You can remove your book from Kindle Select if you so choose, so it isn't as if you're committed there for life — only for three months, at which point you can change your mind and withdraw. A viable strategy is to try putting your book there for the initial three-month period and seeing how well it does, keeping an eye on the number of borrows you get paid for. If it's a tidy sum, you may want to just let it ride. From an administrative point of view, it's much quicker and easier to deal with one avenue of selling your book — Kindle Digital Publishing — than it is to juggle multiple channels, each with their own slightly different requirements. Remember that every minute you spend tweaking and fiddling with your book's sales properties online is a minute not spent on writing the next one...

Some writers like to split the difference between KDP and

going wide, especially when they publish multiple books in a series. They'll place the first book exclusively in Kindle Select, allowing Kindle Unlimited customers to borrow and read it for free, and put the rest of the titles in the series 'wide' — on all of the other available platforms. Note that the other books can still be *sold* on Amazon, they just can't be borrowed and read for free. The hope is that readers will be sufficiently hooked on the first book that they will be willing to pay full price for the others.

Sometimes the gamble pays off, and sometimes it doesn't. When I had four self-published books in print, I decided to experiment with this myself. I enrolled two books from the same series in the Kindle Select program, giving both of them complete exclusivity to Amazon's sales platform, and left them there for six months. At the end of that time, I took them out of Select and published them via Draft2Digital (an excellent site for distributing self-published books to a broader range of sales outlets) and let them ride for another six months, taking my books wide to a bigger potential audience.

The end result: my sales figures from Kindle Select *crushed* the ones from Draft2Digital. Yes, I had sold copies in parts of the world in which Amazon didn't have a significant presence, but it was a relative pittance when compared to the income I had made from the Kindle Select borrows.

I came to the conclusion that on the basis of sales figures alone, the pros of sticking with KDP Select and going all in with them outweighed the benefits of publishing elsewhere, but what about the cons?

Other than losing out on millions of potential readers by welding one's books to KDP Select to the exclusion of all others, there were other drawbacks. Although I was able to publish extracts from my books on my website, richardestep.net, I was prevented from putting more than ten percent of any book online for free, even for reviewing purposes.

A number of authors have run into issues publishing with Kindle Digital Publishing, including the rather disconcerting situation of having their books pulled from publication without any real sort of explanation. This happened to my friend Tim Miller back in 2017, who found one of his already-published titles being withdrawn by Amazon. When he asked why, the answer was oddly vague and generic: "Because it violates our content guidelines."

Unfortunately, when Tim tried to find out exactly *how* the

book violated KDP content guidelines, the company was less than forthcoming. The retraction and banning of the book didn't happen during the actual publishing process. Tim's book had been on the market for over a week and had sold a hundred copies already at the time. (For the full story, see *https://www.timmiller.org/single-post/2017/05/12/Snuff-Film-BANNED)*

Now, Tim writes some pretty graphic horror novels, it has to be said; the sort of thing where chainsaws in eyeballs are par for the course. Yet there are plenty of other extreme horror novels on the market which contain the same types of splatterpunk grotesqueries, and they have yet to be banned.

From what I have been able to gather, the authors whose works are summarily banned tend to be those who publish material containing either a) extreme violence or b) explicit erotica. While that is somewhat understandable, at least from a certain point of view — not one that I personally agree with, but there you go; Jeff Bezos isn't asking me for my opinion — what's worrying is that plenty of books which do contain such material are left untouched. The banning process is nebulous at best, and what's even more worrying is the fact that if they choose to, Amazon reserves the right to shut down your publishing account for reasons of their own choosing, and ban you from ever publishing another book via KDP for the rest of your life.

Some books have been banned because of the cover, either because it contains too much blood, or because the nature of it is deemed too sexually suggestive. It's impossible to say for sure what exactly will arouse the ire of the KDP reviewers, so it is necessary to bear one thing in mind at all times: when you sign exclusively with Amazon, your publishing career is totally and utterly at their mercy.

Caveat emptor. (Let the buyer beware)

The Process

Once you've chosen your platform, it's simply a question of formatting your book to meet their specific requirements. Smashwords, Draft2Digital, and Amazon's KDP all have their commonalities and differences. I've used the latter two, and have no experience with the first.

The preferred way to upload your *paperback* manuscript to KDP is as a properly-formatted PDF, although the website will accept Microsoft Word documents, HTML files, and RTF files.

For the digital (ebook) version, Word documents are also

acceptable (though I've seen these become a little wonky when converted to an ebook file on the website). You can upload .MOBI files, EPUB files, RTF, HTML, even plain text files, if you so choose. My personal preference is to use an EPUB (a generic ebook file format) because it's the most widely-used file type for ebooks. Amazon uses the MOBI format, but not every online publisher does. EPUB works well across the board.

Writing Software

There are many different types of word processing software out there on the market today. I've used Apple Pages on my iPad and liked the intuitive feel of it. Microsoft Word and Pages are both fine for writing magazine articles, blog posts, and short stories; where things get trickier is when it comes to full-length book projects.

Along with many writers, I now tend to use Scrivener. This is a very affordable piece of software, one which allows you to break your project down into chapters, sections, and scenes, reorganizing them at will to suit your purpose. Everything in Scrivener is organized like a binder, allowing you to store photographs and research notes as part of your master project.

One of the best things about the program is its capacity for formatting your text as a PDF, EPUB, MOBI, and many other formats. Your ebook comes out ready to upload, and I always like to preview the EPUB file on my tablet, using the Kindle Reader and iBooks apps to perform quality assurance before finally hitting publish.

There's only one real downside to Scrivener: the learning curve is nothing short of brutal. It is hands down the most challenging piece of software I have ever attempted to master, and coming from somebody who spent eighteen years working in I.T., that's really saying something. Thanks to video tutorials and some snooping around online, I've reached a level of proficiency with Scrivener that allows me to lay out and publish my books in a way that I'm happy with, but a good eighty percent of the features and functionality of the software still eludes me.

When I first began writing, I used Scrivener exclusively on my writing desktop. Now, the manufacturers have released a version for the iPad, which is actually simpler and easier to use, for my money. It connects directly to my Dropbox, ensuring that if I ever make the $1,000 mistake of dropping my tablet onto a concrete apron again, my word count will still be safe and sound.

For my money, Scrivener is hard to beat, standing head and shoulders over its competitors. Just be prepared for a bit of frustration and confusion during your first encounter with it.

Persevere. It'll be worth it in the end.

Title and Cover

"Don't judge a book by its cover."

Bullshit.

People *do* judge a book by its cover. *Always.*

You may have written the greatest masterpiece of twenty-first century literature, an astounding piece of writing that would be a serious contender for the Nobel Prize in Literature — but slap a cheap, home-made cover on the front, and that puppy is going to sink like a stone.

It's worth spending a few minutes cruising around on Amazon, checking out some of the covers. One of the first things you'll discover is that of the bestselling self-published books, none of them have slapped-together covers that look like the enthusiastic daubing of a third grader.

Yes, free cover creator software is out there. You can

certainly save yourself some money by using it. This is usually the very definition of false economy, however. If you splurge on just *one thing* where your book is concerned, it should be the cover.

Think about every time you ever walked into a bookstore, or found yourself browsing the shelves in an airport, at the supermarket, idly scanning the ranks of potential reading material for something to take your fancy. There are so many stories. So many choices.

Two things are going to make you reach out and pick one of those books from the shelf. The first is the title. Indeed, if the books are shelved sideways-on, that's going to be the *only* thing to catch your eye. How catchy is it?

Here are some books whose titles recently grabbed my attention and held it long enough for me to shell out some cash for them.

I Will Teach You to be Rich, by Ramit Sethi. After all, who doesn't want to be rich?

Discipline Equals Freedom, by Jocko Willink. I'll freely admit that the author's name played a big role in my buying this book (I was already aware of his backstory and pedigree. If you're not, you should definitely Google him). This is a short, punchy title, three memorable words and one very simple equation.

Ego is the Enemy, by Ryan Holliday. Like many people, I struggle with my ego. Unchecked ego is the reason for much of the world's misery, and the number one cause of most of the emotional pain we all endure on a daily basis. This title, simple and effective, states a very simple universal truth. Ego really *is* the enemy, and I wanted to find out what Mr. Holliday had to say about it.

Bigger Leaner Stronger: The Simple Science of Building the Ultimate Male Body by Michael Matthews. I'm a 46-year-old man whose waistline is three sizes too big. Damn right I'd like to be bigger (in a muscular sense) leaner and stronger. Those three words sold the book to me on the spot.

All four of these books (and many more besides) sold themselves to me purely on the basis of the title alone. When you choose a title for your book, it's a good idea to make sure that it hasn't already been taken, so enter it into a search engine, then do the same thing over at Amazon.com and BarnesandNoble.com. Although there's no law that says you can't duplicate another book's title and use it yourself, there's a real risk of your book getting lost in the background noise of the search results if the other book is more popular. Can you call your book *The Dark Tower?* Sure. But Stephen

King is going to beat your ass like a drum, thanks to the fact that the first volume of his *Dark Tower* series — 2,953 Amazon reviews and counting — is going to sit at the top of the search results forever. No less a luminary than C.S. Lewis, author of the time-honored Narnia series, also wrote a book by that name. It only has 55 reviews on Amazon.com, and sits nine places down on the search list, after all of Mr. King's *Dark Tower* books. Stephen King and C.S. Lewis are almost certainly guaranteed to outsell you, so why handicap yourself in this way? Pick a fresh, unique title for your book, one that will jump out and captivate the potential reader, even if they only see the spine.

A good title is short, punchy, and gets into your head. It either lets the reader infer exactly what the book is going to be about (*Haunted Healthcare*) or on the flip side, injects an air of mystery that will — hopefully — make them want to learn more. That was my rationale for titling my book about the haunting of a former residential nursing facility *The Devil's Coming to Get Me*. My hope was that a potential reader would think: "The Devil — as in, *literally* the Devil, is coming to get somebody? Who? Why? I have to read this book to find out!"

Put some serious consideration into the title of your book.

A longer subtitle is also a good idea, as it will increase the book's searchability within the Kindle store. More on this later.

Back in the early stages of planning your book, as you were browsing your way through the various Amazon categories and subcategories pertaining to the subject you wanted to write about, you should have been exposed to a large number of covers. Which ones caught your eye, and why? What was it about them (other than the ranking of that particular book in the sales chart) that caused you to stop, click, and take a closer look?

Creating a knockout book cover is nothing less than an art form in itself, and unless you happen to be a first-rate graphic designer and artist yourself, it's one best left to the professionals. A great cover is simplistic, without being *too* simple, containing enough detail to catch the eye but without looking cluttered. The words of the title, subtitle, and author's name have to stand out from the background art, without being too obtrusive.

Remember that one avenue of selling your book involves the 'also bought.' Amazon has a vested interest in showing you books that it thinks you will want to buy. As such, when you click on any given book title, scrolling down the page a little way will show you the covers of books that other purchasers of that particular title have also bought. Those cover images will be small, a little bigger than thumbnails, so if your book is going to appear as one of some other writer's also boughts, you want it to look clean and attractive even when smooshed down to a fraction of its normal size.

Above all else, the cover has to fit with the theme of the book. If you have written a romance novel, it shouldn't contain images of blood, death, fire and brimstone — unless your story takes place in Hell, of course. (Come to think of it, that sounds like a great idea for a novel — a romance set in Hell. Hmmm...)

The books I write are primarily paranormal nonfiction. Ghosts and haunted houses are the order of the day, sometimes with a side order of UFOs or some other bizarre phenomenon. Not one of those covers is bright, sunny, and cheerful. Instead, they contain ramshackle old houses, graveyards, castles, and mysterious phantom figures prowling through dark and shadowy hallways. The reader knows exactly what they're going to get when they look inside, without even looking at the title or the descriptive copy on the back. They're ghost books, and the artwork practically *screams* 'ghost book!'

When it comes to creating a near-perfect book cover, a good artist/graphic designer really is worth their weight in gold. For the cover of my first self-published book, *The Beast of Mysore,* I used the services of *www.99designs.com.* I had heard about them via one of my favorite writing podcasts, *The Self-Publishing Podcast* (now sadly ended) and thought that their business model was an excellent idea.

Essentially, the idea behind a 99Designs project was for me to write down exactly what I was looking for: in this case, the cover of a horror/history/fantasy novel, one which was heavily focused on vampires. Artists and designers would then put together their best conceptual cover designs, competing against one another for the top spot. Of those, I selected a handful whose designs I really liked, and suggested one or two refinements that I'd like to see.

After taking my feedback on board, the designers went away and made the modifications I'd requested. Of those, I picked the one that I liked best, and awarded the contract to him. He made a couple of very minor tweaks to the artwork, then lo and behold, that became the final cover for my book.

All in all, this cost me $299, which was a great price to pay for a professional quality book cover. I was very happy with the end result, but there were a couple of problems along the way.

Things got a little embarrassing when one of the designers who had made it through to the penultimate phase of the competition, only to be passed over in favor of the winner, wrote to me and demanded to know just what, exactly, was wrong with *his* artwork? I could totally see his point: after pouring what I can only assume were several hours' worth of inspiration and effort into the project, only to see it shot down at the final hurdle, he was quite understandably rather pissed off. But those were the rules of the game.

Competitions worked in just that way, something he'd agreed to when he signed up to be a part of it. His artwork wasn't bad at all; in fact, it was of very decent quality, and if the winner hadn't put in such a strong performance, I would probably have been happy to have it grace the cover of my book.

Unfortunately, competitions like this are a Darwinian process. There can be only one winner, which means that somebody, obviously, has to be on the losing side. I really didn't like the idea of pitting talented, hard-working artists against one another in what had started to feel like a miniature version of *The Hunger Games*. Feeling obligated to answer his questions, I wrote back and explained my reasoning, but for him, that only seemed to rub salt into the wound. It made me question my desire to ever want to do something like this again.

As things turned out, the company hosting the competition took a sizable share of that $299 fee — understandable, as they were providing the platform which connected me with the potential cover designers. But I would much rather have put all of that money straight into the pocket of the designer himself.

For future books, I would eventually transition to working directly with one graphic designer and cutting out the middle man. We cultivated a relationship based upon mutual respect and good communication. It's a model that works very well for me to this day. The same designer has produced the covers for all of my self-published books, and has developed a fundamental understanding of their theme. He knocks it out of the park every time, usually on the very first attempt. There are usually one or two minor tweaks I ask for on a cover design, but for the most part, the designs require very little in the way of modification before going to print.

I make a point of paying him promptly, just as soon as I approve a cover design. For one flat fee, he provides me with a full front-and-back paperback book cover, a single-sheet cover for an ebook, and a square cover formatted for the *Audible.com* audiobook edition. Three covers for the price of one. In fact, he designed the cover for the book that you are currently reading or listening to.

Once your cover is set in stone, it's time to write a little sales copy. This will be a few lines of text that will serve as the book's description when a potential customer clicks on the title. Many authors use the text from the back cover of the paperback edition, two or three paragraphs which attempt to hook the reader on the book's premise, in the hope that they will want to read more. You have just a few short lines to do this, so it is worth poring over the sales copy, tinkering with the flow of words until you are satisfied that it is the best it can possibly be. This will usually be the reader's first exposure to your style of writing. If you do your job well, it won't be the last.

Pricing

Ah, pricing. One of the most contentious, talked-about subjects among self-published authors, particularly when it comes to the Kindle sales platform. Let's try and demystify things a little.

There are basically two royalty share options when you publish your book with KDP: 35% and 70%. Only a fool would choose 35%, right? Not necessarily. In order to get the 70% option, you have to price your book between $2.99 and $9.99. Anything that falls outside those parameters (cheaper than $2.99 or more expensive than $9.99) can only earn 35%.

The message that Amazon is sending to its KDP writers is very clear: if you want to maximize profit, don't price your books too low or too high. That isn't to say that nothing gets published outside the $2.99-$9.99 sweet spot. A lot of short stories are selling for $0.99 or $1.99, including some of my own. It doesn't seem fair to me to ask for more than a dollar or two for something that only adds up to a few thousand words. That may be an old-fashioned approach for me to take, but as a purchaser of books in addition to being a seller, I have a very definite notion of what constitutes good value for money. Your opinion may differ, and that's perfectly okay. What it really comes down to, at the end of the day, is just how much money a given customer is willing to pay for what you've written.

I must point out again that many readers are going to weigh the cost of your book against the number of pages that it contains, to work out whether (in their minds, at least) it seems to be value for money. This happens with ebooks and hard copies. Does $2.99, a very common price point for many ebooks, seem worth it for something that is only 47 pages long? Again, that's something that each individual reader will decide for themselves.

This is where Kindle Unlimited really shines, because the KU reader doesn't care about the sale price for your book if it's enrolled in the KDP Select program. Their perception is that they are reading for free, whereas you, the writer, are getting paid for each page that is read. A customer may balk at paying $9.99 for your title, but will happily borrow it and start reading away if they can do so as part of their ten-book Kindle Unlimited allowance — another good argument for enrolling your titles in KDP Select.

Categories and Keywords

We spoke earlier about the importance of Amazon categories, and how helpful it can be, in terms of increased visibility and sales, for your book to hit the top 100 chart for its given subcategory.

One of the things I tend to agonize over is the subject of

KEYWORDS. These are phrases which Amazon allows you to enter for each book that you publish. You have an allowance of just seven keywords, so it pays to use them wisely. They determine how easily readers that are punching in search phrases, such as *Haunted Houses* or *Demonic Entities*, are able to find your book.

Actually, the term key*words* is a little misleading, because each keyword can actually be a sentence up to fifty characters long. PHANTOMS DEMONS HEADLESS HORSEMEN POLTERGEISTS SPOOKS would be a perfectly valid, single keyword, for example, leaving you with six more to use up on other descriptive phrases.

Be sure to get the most bang for your buck when it comes to keywords by making them somewhat diverse (cast as wide a net as you reasonably can) while at the same time, ensuring that they reflect a true representation of your book.

As someone who is primarily an author of paranormal non-fiction, I frequently use keywords such as GHOSTS, GHOSTLY, HAUNTED, HAUNTING, PARANORMAL, POLTERGEIST, SPIRIT, DEMONIC (yes, I know — eye roll) POSSESSION, ENTITIES, and a host of similar variations. It is fair to say that any reader searching for these words is going to be a good fit for the type of books I write.

The two books I have authored on the subject of the ghosts of Gettysburg also use the keywords AMERICAN CIVIL WAR, BATTLE OF GETTYSBURG, CAVALRY BATTLE, and other similar phrases relating to the war of 1861-1865.

If, on the other hand, I add keywords such as ACTION, MILITARY THRILLER, SPY, ESPIONAGE, ROMANCE, LOVE STORY, EPIC FANTASY, or countless others that don't truly represent the contents of my books, I am going to piss off any reader who purchases one of them with the expectation of finding those things inside.

Tailor your keywords to the key concepts and subjects contained in your book, and it's hard to go wrong. Use all seven, and make sure you fill them up. GHOSTS AMERICAN CIVIL WAR UNION CONFEDERATE would be a great keyword for *The Fairfield Haunting* or *The Farnsworth House Haunting,* my two Gettysburg titles. They would grossly misrepresent either of my *Haunted Healthcare* books.

CHAPTER SEVENTEEN

Marketing and Branding

Although my primary goal in writing this book was to help aspiring authors to write, complete, and publish their first book, the title, *Building the Write Life*, was also intended to convey something broader: my desire to assist those brave souls who, rather than stopping with a single book release, want to turn writing into a long term prospect.

At this point in your writing journey, your first book should either be in release, or well on the way to being so. Whether you have placed it with a traditional publishing house, or chosen to release it yourself, let's assume that you have taken care of book number one, and are ready to think about the next step on the path.

The majority of this section will talk about marketing and branding. Doing those two things correctly — and they are, in my experience, both inextricably intertwined — can make all the difference between having a healthy, viable publishing career, and fading away into obscurity, with dwindling sales and loss of interest from your reading audience.

Your Brand

According to that paragon of accuracy, Wikipedia, a brand can be defined as: "a name, term, design, symbol or any other feature that identifies one seller's good or service as distinct from those of other sellers."

As definitions go, it's as good as any, I suppose. Yet the word *brand* has come to take on a variety of meanings. For our purposes, I'm going to define it as meaning 'the thing or things that render the products of your writing unique.'

Once readers find an author whose work they like, they tend to develop certain expectations. Stephen King's brand, for the longest time, was that of dark, creepy chiller mixed with blood-soaked horror, and he continued in that literary vein — pun very much intended — for quite some time. *Carrie* begat *Salem's Lot*, which begat *The Shining,* which begat *The Stand,* which begat *The Dead Zone*, and so on, and so on...

King's readers knew what to expect each time one of his bestsellers hit the shelves: macabre horror stories that would keep them awake at night. Once he had hit his stride, however, King began to branch out, deviating from his established formula into the realm of fantasy, with books such as *The Talisman, The Eyes of the Dragon,* and *The Dark Tower* series. Because he had taken the time to build up the Stephen King brand, gaining a loyal fanbase along the way, those readers had enough trust in his writing chops to go along with him on those new tangents.

Stephen King is still, to this day, his own brand. Although his books now defy easy categorization, ranging as they do across multiple different genres, there is always something indefinably *Kingish* about them.

How are you going to build your own distinctive brand? It all begins with writing style. It will take a while for you to find your writing voice, as it were, but once you do, the prose will begin to fly across the page. It's common for writers to be all over the place, stylistically speaking, in the early stages of their career, but once you gain confidence as a writer, your manuscripts will start to take on that unique voice which sets you apart from your peers.

Genre and category play a significant role too. I've spent the past four years writing about ghosts and hauntings. I deviated a little by writing a book about UFOs, which didn't seem too far from my usual bailiwick, and by now I have a fairly lengthy mailing list of regular readers who like to read about the spooky places I visit and investigate.

After publishing a book about the haunting of a serial killer's house *(The Horrors of Fox Hollow Farm)* I was offered a contract to write a book about serial killers — *just* serial killers. No ghosts involved. Nothing paranormal in any way, shape, or form. The prospect is an exciting one; what author doesn't want to branch out into pastures new, every once in a while? It's not to say that I'm giving up the ghost (again, pun very much intended) because the paranormal is and always will be my first love, in literary terms. But now that I have been fortunate enough to attract a loyal readership, it is my firm hope that a large number of them will follow me across into this new genre of non-fiction writing, much as Stephen King's readers stuck with him when he started putting out fantasy books.

After all, they're my tribe.

Find Your Tribe

The word 'tribe' may conjure up images of people living in a rain forest or on a savanna somewhere, but in the context of creative writing, it means something entirely different.

Modern society is becoming increasingly fractured. Despite our having round-the-clock access to a bewildering mountain of data, ranging from the 24-hour news cycle to our having the ability to reach out and communicate with others around the globe in the blink of an eye, it is safe to say that we, as human beings, have never felt so isolated and alone.

Welcome to the twenty-first century.

One response to this growing sense of social isolation that we all seem to feel, to a greater or a lesser degree, has been the emergence of tribal culture. Thanks to the ubiquity of digital communication, finding somebody who shares a similar interest or passion that you do, has never been easier.

People from all across the globe band together to carry out raids in *World of Warcraft.* A nine-year-old kid from Zurich can machine-gun a middle-aged guy in Colorado while playing an on-line shooter such as *Rainbow Six: Siege* on XBox Live (not that I'm bitter, damn it!). Every day, people strike up friendships with those they have never physically met in person, thanks to Facebook and other social media sites. Former strangers become fast friends without letting a minor detail such as geography get in the way.

Whatever you're a fan of, from *Star Wars* to *My Little Pony,* the chances are there's a group of people who are deeply passionate about that very same thing.

They are your tribe. People who share your specific weird, and will welcome you unquestioningly into their circle.

When it comes to publishing, these people are the natural audience for your book. Your area of expertise, no matter what it happens to be, also happens to be their personal passion. In my case, people who like to spend their free nights poking around abandoned, supposedly haunted old buildings, are my tribe...and the core audience for my books, to boot.

The truth is, I'd hang out with these people every chance I got, whether they happened to buy my books or not. I had been investigating claims of ghosts and hauntings for twenty years before ever sitting down to write a book, and in that time, I met many wonderful people, most of them with a similar mind set to my own, who liked to do the same thing. We spoke the same language, went to the same places, and got excited about the same things.

My tribe.

Now, they're the same people that keep my books in the Amazon charts, supporting my writing, cheering me on, and giving honest feedback. They're not shy about telling me what they liked and didn't like about any given book, but they keep coming back for more, picking up my latest book on the day it is released. (If you're reading this, my friends, you know who you are — and I love you for helping me do what I do).

Finding your tribe is actually fairly easy. They'll most likely be members of the same Facebook groups as you, sharing and commenting on the same posts. If you go to conventions, seminars, or expos, you'll find them there, wandering the same aisles and listening to the same speakers as you.

Embrace these people. They are your tribe.

Once you start writing and publishing, you will naturally attract those types of people to you. It's important to engage with your tribe regularly. Letting them know that you have a new book coming out is important, yes, but what's *more* important is to answer their questions and comments in a timely manner. Your readers part with hard-earned money in exchange for the right to read your books. They deserve to have you stay engaged with them (maintaining appropriate boundaries, of course) and to have some kind of open communication channel with you.

It's pretty much essential for you to get a web site. Readers expect an author to have some sort of online presence, and you don't necessarily have to shell out a lot of money to make it happen. One of the ways to get the best bang for your buck is a Wordpress site, one of the more basic (but still professional-looking) varieties of web site.

For a fairly modest fee, it's possible to purchase a domain name that maps to your own name — in my case, *richardestep.net* — and connect your site to it. The site forms a central hub for information about you, your books, and things such as radio show/podcast appearances, book signings, future releases, and anything else pertinent to your writing life that you might want to share.

I use my site to host a blog, one which I need to be a lot more diligent about keeping updated with regular posts. Readers use it to comment, ask questions, or just generally stop by and say hello. It also contains an email address, which allows them to contact me personally (*not* my personal email address — this one is expressly set aside for communicating with my fans and readers) and a means of signing up for my email list.

For many writers, the idea of starting up an email list is right up there with watching paint dry in terms of the fun factor involved. Yet it's hard to overstate the importance of setting one up. There are a couple of reasons for this.

Firstly, in an age when everybody is deluged with

unsolicited spam on a daily basis, the idea of a reader voluntarily sharing their email address with a favorite writer is an act of trust, one that — at the risk of sounding saccharine — bonds the two of them together. It basically says, "Hey, I like your stuff so much that I'll let you email me on a regular basis and tell me when you have a new book coming out, or something cool is going on." That's no small thing.

Secondly, there's a well-documented correlation between maintaining an active email list and increased book sales. Remember that these are the people who *want* to hear from you. They signed up for you to do just that. If they don't want to buy your next book, who does?

The people on an author's email list tend to be their biggest and more hardcore fans. As such, they deserve respect and a healthy amount of attention. Loyalty like that should count for something, after all.

The last thing I want to cover on the subject of web sites is that of blogging. In my view, it's a good tool for communicating with your readers, but one to be used sparingly.

How can too much blogging be a bad thing? Because blog entries can easily run to a thousand words or more, and that can really cut into your daily word count. If you're not careful, writing a daily blog entry can become a regular time suck, draining your creative juices and sapping your will to write. A great rule to live by is this: time spent writing blogs, promotional pieces, emails, letters, or anything else of an administrative nature, should *never* count as part of your daily word count. If you hammer out a thousand-word blog, give yourself a pat on the back — but don't let it excuse you from hitting your daily five hundred, thousand, or whatever target you set for yourself.

Reviews

There are few things more frustrating, maddening, and sometimes, downright glorious to a writer than a book review. They are the ultimate double-edged sword.

On the one hand, good reviews are the lifeblood of book sales; the more you have, the more likely that casually browsing customer is to hand over their money, which is especially important if you are an unknown quantity to them; on the other, nothing can ruin a writer's day faster than a shitty review. *Nothing*.

When it comes to reviews, the conventional wisdom holds

that you shouldn't let them get you down or prey on your mind.

While I agree in principle, the fact of the matter is that this is far easier said than done. A writer labors over their manuscript for weeks, months, sometimes *years* at a time. Try as we might, we almost always grow emotionally attached to them. They become a part of us, and we see them as a reflection of our value, our sense of self-worth. To have somebody come along and puncture our bubble can be excruciatingly painful, no matter how much we might try to convince ourselves otherwise.

Authors need to be thick-skinned, it is true; yet no matter how crusty and cantankerous we may appear to be on the outside, the vast majority of us still crave one thing: acceptance of our work. We want somebody to read the words we have toiled over, and we want that somebody to *like* them.

I can get ten great reviews on a book and one absolute stinker. Which do I focus on? You guessed it...

They say that no love can ever quite compare with your first love. In the publishing world, my first love was *In Search of the Paranormal. Yes,* it has its flaws, and if I had the chance to write it all over again, there are definitely some changes I'd make, but by and large, I'm very fond of that book. I'm also, rightly or wrongly, proud of it. It was the book that proved I was able to write prose to a publishable standard.

Currently, it has 33 reviews on Amazon. 73% of them are 5-star. 24% of them are 4-star. Some of the phrases used by reviewers genuinely moved me, such as *"Mr. Estep has a writing style that is a reader-friendly breath of fresh air,"* and *"I highly recommend these stories to anyone who is interested in tales of ghosts and hauntings and also to those who just enjoy an exciting adventure told by a master storyteller!"* I really appreciate the fact that these readers took time out of their day to say such kind things about my work.

And then it lands: that 2-star review, sticking out amongst the 4- and 5-stars like a sore thumb.

I found it boring and drug on and on. I'm baffled by all the 5 stars? Am I missing something? Nothing happens...hardly anything substantiated. I found it boring and drug on and on. Traipsing around fields at night with thermos' full of tea didn't cut it. A bang/crash here and there...yawn. On to the next.

On reading it, my first reaction came from the gut, not

from the head; a visceral, almost palpable surge of anger. Who were to criticize the book I had worked so damn hard on for months of my life?

The answer, of course, is 'a paying customer.' This person had spent their hard-earned money in order to purchase *In Search of the Paranormal.* They were obviously hoping for something more exciting and action packed. The book is undeniably a slow burn; in fact, one of my favorite reviews said that the reviewer "loved how much paranormal there *isn't* in this book."

The cover design, which was beautifully done by the publishing house art department, teases a dark and haunting book. That was what I had set out to write. The reviewer was disappointed that, in their opinion, the story inside didn't live up to that promise. And do you know what? Perhaps they're right.

I don't think for a moment that the reviewer set out to ruin my day. My belief is that they wanted to share a frank and honest opinion about a book that had disappointed them. I had to remind myself rather firmly that they were perfectly entitled to their point of view, and to share it with the rest of the world. We've all read books that disappointed us. Some, I found so dreary that I couldn't finish, abandoning them before reaching the half way point. So, who the hell was *I* to judge?

One of the hard truths about being a writer is this: whenever you put your writing out there into the world for all to see, people are going to have opinions about it. Some will love it. Some will be ambivalent. Others will hate it.

Hate it.

The 1-star reviews are the worst. This is the lowest score that a book can possibly get. Each one cuts you and throbs, getting more and more painful with every passing word.

This is, quite possibly, the worst written book I have ever read! exclaims an anonymous Amazon customer in their review of my book, *The Devil's Coming to Get Me: The Haunting of Malvern Manor* – *and that's saying something because I've read a ton of books! This book sounded promising, the intro parts sounded interesting and I was looking forward to reading all about the "ghostly adventures" happening at this place.*

My gut was churning as I scanned through this diatribe, just knowing that the worst was still to come. I wasn't wrong.

Then I got to the first chapter. I could not read it. It was written in the weirdest format I've ever seen, like listening to a person high on crack telling a story.

Ouch ouch ouch ouch *ouch.*

So many super quick, run on sentences and jumping from this person to that person and back again, I didn't even know who these people being talked about were! There was such a rapid fire pace and I don't know why? What is the rush to get the words out so quickly?

The reviewer then proceeds to school me on how I should have written the book.

Just tell the story calmly and let the thing flow naturally. You're not on a tv show, you're supposed to be writing a book, you need to learn how to manage your pace. Maybe next time get a ghost writer? Or just don't write at all, it's not your forte.

Boom.

Just don't write at all. It's not your forte.

Try to put yourself in my shoes for a minute, dear reader, and imagine what it must have felt like to read those words. This goes beyond constructive criticism — there's little constructive about the entire piece, other than telling me to slow down and manage my pace, perhaps. This is nothing less than spite.

The old cliches suddenly all came true at once. I could feel my heart pounding in my chest, causing my pulse to throb at my temple. My fists clenched and unclenched. Who the hell was this, and how *dare* they say nasty stuff like this to me?

Unlike the 2-star reviewer of *In Search of the Paranormal,* this person had no desire to pull any punches whatsoever. They hadn't a care in the world with regard to how hurtful their comments were; in fact, I suspect that if they had known the amount of emotional pain their review had caused me — particularly that vicious final sentence — they would have taken a perverse joy from the fact.

It was tempting — oh, so *very* tempting — to bash out a reply to this hateful individual, rebutting their comments one by one, and making a few pointed remarks about their manners, or lack thereof.

Fortunately, common sense prevailed.

I had to step away from my desk and take a walk, in order to calm down and clear my head. Gradually, a sense of perspective returned. I reminded myself of the golden rule of dealing with Internet comments: Do not feed the trolls.

Some people are simply hateful, spiteful, judgmental individuals. Such people would never dare say to a person's face the things that they are willing to write online, hiding behind the cloak of anonymity. That's a form of cowardice.

Clicking on the profile link for "Amazon Customer" I found that he or she seemed to like nothing more than to dish out negative reviews, which comprised about 75% of them. No, not just negative...*harsh* reviews. That was apparent from some of the titles of their other book reviews.

Should be illegal! declared one. *Yet another poorly written unprofessional self published piece of garbage. How many more can we expect from this "author?" This kind of writing should be illegal!*

One star.

I kept scrolling.

Don't quit your day job! Such a poorly written amateurish endeavor! This is obviously a self published author and the previous reviews have been written by friends and relatives, I couldn't even finish the book. leave it to the professionals honey and don't quit your day job — if you even have one.

One star.

It was beginning to look as though I had gotten off lightly. A pattern was also starting to appear. "Amazon Customer" apparently had a thing against self-published books, and loved to give life coaching advice to those who enjoyed writing them...advice of the most condescending and spiteful kind.

On and on it went. Another paranormal book was "boring, not scary," and the 1-star review ended with a summary: "It is poorly written, extremely boring, and I wish I'd never purchased it."

I suspected that the author wished the same thing. He probably wasn't too upset though, because the book in question had a total of 1,440 reviews, and a 4-star average, which meant that the vast majority of readers really liked it. 64% of them were 5-star reviews. Only 5% were 1-star. I found it highly unlikely that this was a poorly written book.

After reviewing the long string of negativity on this anonymous reviewer's profile, a number of things became clear to me. Firstly, this was by no means a personal attack against me. A number of other self-published authors were also in the cross-hairs of "Amazon Customer." *All* of our books were poorly written, in the eyes of this reviewer.

Secondly, this type of shrewish individual can be found everywhere. In the school playground, in the workplace, out in public…but most especially on the Internet, where it's likely that nobody is going to hold them accountable for the things they say. Some people just love nothing more than to tear others down, particularly when they put their creation out there in the public eye for all to see — and judge.

Never read the reviews, some people say. In a perfect world, we'd all have that level of discipline, but I certainly don't, and I doubt that you do either. It's a very human thing, this wanting to put our art out into the world and see what our fellow human beings make of it.

Unfortunately, we're not always emotionally prepared for the consequences.

What's needed is a sense of perspective. Every book ever published — literally *every* book — has gotten its share of hate.

For starters, it's good to remember that when you get a terrible review, you find yourself in the best of company. Stephen King, the master of the macabre, gets his fair share (*dull*, says a one word, 1-star review of *Salem's Lot*, arguably the greatest vampire novel ever written).

Harry Potter and the Sorcerer's Stone, one of the widely-acknowledged classics of children's fantasy literature, gets 1 star because, in the eloquent words of a reviewer whose name I won't repeat, *"It's witchcraft!"* A terrible review, written because J.K. Rowling's imagination doesn't jive with the reviewer's personal philosophy. One wonders if he even read the book.

As for J.R.R. Tolkien's timeless masterpiece *The Lord of*

the Rings, it's nothing more than a "great book if you want to take a nap, according to one of its 1-star reviews.

You may be one hell of a writer, but the chances are that you're no King, Rowling, or Tolkien, and that's okay. Few of us are. These giants of the literary field all get bad reviews to this very day. I figure that if three of the biggest names in fiction get raked over the coals, then a writer such as myself, who isn't even within sight of the same ballpark as them, has no real right to complain if the odd stinker comes along.

Now, don't get me wrong here: if the *majority* of your reviews are 1 and 2-star, you might want to look at your material with a more critical eye. It's unlikely that all of those readers are wrong. Look for commonalities among the critical points, and see if there's something you can fix. It may be worth pulling the book for a while, reworking it, and publishing it again later, once it's in better shape.

There's a school of thought which says that the occasional poor review actually does your book more good than harm, and so we should be grateful for them. Some customers are put off when they see nothing but positive reviews, almost as if the book is too good to be true, somehow. Seeing one or two critical reviews can be reassuring.

The one thing you must never, *ever* do, is respond to a

negative reviewer. No matter how antagonistic they are being, no matter how cruel and petty the review is, *do not return fire.* One hundred percent of the time, the author that chooses to do this end up looking as bad as, if not even worse than, the reviewer that goaded them into doing so.

Other than a brief period of righteous self-indignation, which may or may not feel satisfying, there's no upside to getting into it with a negative reviewer. They have nothing to lose. The writer, on the other hand, has his or her image at stake. It can very easily be perceived as the almighty author picking on somebody who had the temerity to dislike their work. If that's how people start see you, it can be tough to come back from a misperception like that. The momentary surge of satisfaction you may feel will soon be drowned out by the damage that is done to your reputation.

Far better to swallow your pride, do whatever it takes to calm yourself down, and do something productive — by which I mean, sit down at the keyboard and pour all of those words you were planning to unleash on your nemesis into your next manuscript instead.

At the end of the day, you're getting paid to do what you love: write books. Chances are that the small-minded, hit and run reviewer never will.

Asking for Reviews

There's a certain etiquette involved when it comes to asking for reviews. The rule of thumb seems to be that it is perfectly okay to request reviews from your readers every once in a while, but it is never acceptable to badger them into leaving one.

At the end of each book, I thank the reader for having parted with their hard-earned money in order to read it, and then respectfully ask them to rate the book on Amazon. By my estimation, less than 5% actually go out and do so. Not that there's anything wrong with that. We all hate those pop-up surveys and emails inviting us to share our opinions about a recently-purchased product or service, don't we? A minor irritation at best, and a genuine pain in the ass at worst.

I'm always genuinely grateful when a reader chooses to take time out of their day to rate my book and leave me a review. It often shows that they were sufficiently pleased by the reading experience to want to share it with other readers — high praise indeed.

I try very hard never to pressure readers into doing so, however. Every once in a while — usually about every six months or so — I'll put out a polite request via my Facebook author page, asking my followers to please consider leaving me a review. Each time, ten or twelve new reviews spring up on various books I have written. Those reviews mount up over time. While I can't lay claim to any specific insider knowledge on the subject, it is well known that the more positive reviews a book has, the more likely a reader is to take a chance on it.

On occasion, it's okay to ask your readership to rate your book, if they are willing to do so. Over the space of a year or two, you'll soon have a healthy number of them accumulated. Slow and steady always wins this particular race.

CHAPTER EIGHTEEN

A Larger World

"That's good. You've taken your first step into a larger world." — Obi Wan Kenobi, *Star Wars Episode IV: A New Hope.*

Your first book is out there in the world. Hopefully it's selling well, although even under the best circumstances, that's by no means a given. Be prepared for it to descend into relative obscurity fairly quickly, despite your very best efforts.

You can launch a Facebook ad campaign, enlist your friends, family members, and followers on social media to spread the word, and even apply for an ad spot with Bookbub (one of the most widespread, effective book sales tools on the market today)...you can do all that and more, but the cold, hard truth of the matter is that most books are here today and gone tomorrow. Even a traditionally published book will be little more than an afterthought once a few months have passed by, in many cases.

For some writers, that will be enough. Having written and

published one book in their lifetime will provide satisfaction aplenty. This is a genuine achievement, the sort of thing that few people ever manage to achieve. Stopping there is perfectly fine.

I'm speaking now to those writers who want to keep going, to push beyond that first book and keep going, to see what lies beyond it.

To build themselves the write life.

A Bigger Footprint

There's one thing that most successful writers have in common. They write a lot, and they publish a lot.

They are, in a word, prolific. Quantity has a quality all of its own, and while I'm not advocating that you churn out a constant stream of crap, I do believe that there are significant benefits to writing consistently. For starters, most of a writer's early work is their weakest. It was certainly true in my case, and tends to be true for others. As long as you're paying attention and learning from the process, each short story, novel, or book should be better than the last. It's a journey of constant improvement, which is one of the joys of the thing, as well as a source of frustration. We're so impatient to rev it up and get through the writing process that sometimes, it's easy for us to forget to just sit back and enjoy the ride.

Think of each publication you put out there as a footprint, your unique imprint on the publishing landscape. One single footprint is easy to miss in the mass of background noise that constitutes Amazon's ocean of available books.

The solution is to expand your footprint.

Think of each different aspect of your title as a way of making that footprint bigger. The ebook is the initial footprint. Putting out a paperback version makes it bigger, reaching out to that significant readership that flatly refuses to read anything digitally. Those are the people that love the feel of a physical book in their hands, the smell of it, the act of turning the pages. There are many people out there that will never give up their softcovers or hardbacks, and this is the only way to reach them.

You can expand your reach even further by releasing an audio version of your book. More and more readers are choosing this as their preferred method of enjoying books while they work out or commute to work. It's hard to beat the Audiobook Creation eXchange, or ACX, as the best platform for doing so, at least for a new indie author. This is an Amazon-owned company that allows authors to sell audiobooks via Amazon.com, Audible.com, and iTunes.

There are a number of different production options available. If you're willing to invest some time, effort, and money, you can buy the necessary equipment to record, edit, and release the book yourself. That's what my friend, fellow paranormal nonfiction author E.E. Bensen does. Although it can be time-consuming and labor-intensive, this method has the benefit of allowing the author to keep all of the royalties (the percentage varies with the number of units sold).

I tried the do-it-yourself method, with less than stellar results. Caught up in a spirit of unfounded optimism that came out of nowhere, I purchased a professional-quality microphone, complete with stabilizing arm. For recording software, I used Audacity, which has the tremendous virtue of being free. Then, after a little online research on the subject of how to set up an ad hoc recording booth, I draped some towels from hangers in my walk-in bedroom closet and sat down to record the first chapter of *In Search of the Paranormal*.

It's only when you have a set of high quality, noise canceling headphones that you come to appreciate just how *loud* your own home is. I live a block away from a fairly busy street. Sitting on my couch, even without the TV on, you'd never know it. The most you can hear is the quiet hum of the air conditioning unit during the summer, and the constant burbling of an indoor fountain that sits on a kitchen shelf, primarily for the amusement of our cats — who are much more interested in the box it came in.

Things change when the headphones go on. The *slightest* ambient noise — every microscopic creak, a car passing by on the street outside, or a dog scratching its ear — can be heard with obnoxious clarity. A Cessna flying overhead at 7,000 feet sounds like an air raid to a high-fidelity mic. The air horn of a train crossing the railroad tracks three miles away is magnified, becoming something akin to the horns sounding at the Battle of Jericho.

ACX has some hard and fast rules that pertain to the quality of audio recordings they will accept for publication. This is most definitely a good thing; it prevents the audio books we spend our hard-earned credits on from sounding as if they were recorded inside a tin can. Unfortunately, it requires a lot more time and effort than I was willing to put in. When I ran a quality-checking plug-in through Audacity, my raw audio file was woefully sub-par when compared to the ACX requirements. Even after I purchased some studio-quality acoustic dampening foam and covered the walls with it, there was no escaping the conclusion that my house was just too damned noisy.

After whining about it to E.E. Bensen, who did me the courtesy of not rolling his eyes or telling me to put a sock in it, he shared the secret of his own success with me. He had recorded his own books for ACX at home, after constructing a purpose-built sound booth in his basement. I looked at photos of it on his phone and let out an appreciative whistle. The man was a better carpenter than I'll ever be. I had neither the time, the talent, or frankly the desire to do that myself.

"Do you want me to just record your book for you, man?" he asked me. Having narrated not only his own books for ACX but also those of several other authors, he knew all the ins and outs of the business. I gratefully accepted his offer.

We worked together under ACX's royalty sharing option, in which a producer/narrator — in this case, E.E. — takes an author's book and turns it into a professional-quality audio book. The profits are split 50/50 between the two of us. I saw this as the ultimate win/win situation. My book, *The Fairfield Haunting: On the Gettysburg Ghost Trail* was selling nicely in both paperback and digital formats, but getting an audio version off the ground was a bigger hassle than I was prepared to deal with. Life's too short to do stuff you hate, I reasoned, and the recording/narration process was one of the most frustrating things I had encountered in a long time.

Frankly, I knew that my valuable time was better spent on writing than sitting in front of a microphone. After my discouraging early experiences, I doubted that I would ever see the recording process through to completion, even if I could somehow get the audio files up to ACX's lofty standards. Yes, by going in on a 50/50 royalty split, I was giving away half of my earnings — but keeping half of something is better than having all of nothing.

I didn't have to lift a finger during the recording process. All that I needed to do was approve the final recording, and boom, there it was — a fresh edition of my work, available for purchase on the audio market. The only thing I had to do was collect the revenue each month.

It's important for me to point out that, before you make a foray into the world of ACX or some other audio sales platform, you should revise your expectations of how much money you're going to make. Although some audiobooks sell very well indeed, a lot of smaller releases (such as those by newer indie authors) sell only a handful of units each month. To give you a sense of perspective, in the space of exactly one year, *The Fairfield Haunting* sold 86 copies. *Haunted Healthcare,* which consistently outsells *Fairfield* in both digital and paperback formats, sold 139 copies in just four months. With profit sharing, my audio releases — of which I currently have three books and a short story — net me somewhere between $75 and $100 a month. Hardly enough to write home about, you may say, but it is absolutely *free* money. I don't do a thing to earn it, other than turn over a manuscript to a narrator/producer. As more books hit the market this way, that amount will get bigger, continuing to rise as my 'footprint' gets bigger.

One of my traditional publishers has allowed me to keep the audio rights to my books. Others have not. I retain complete audio copyright to all of my self-published books, and will continue to release them on a regular basis. Even for the newly-published writer, it's well worth seeing what ACX has to offer you.

It's the journey, not the destination

"The harder I work, the luckier I get." This particular quote has been attributed to a number of different people, usually with a slight variation in each case. No matter who actually said it, it's a principle that I have found to be true throughout my entire life, one of those guiding stars that you can reliably chart a course by.

In addition to the fun and satisfaction that it has given me along the way, my publishing journey has opened a lot of side doors, and sent me on excursions that I wouldn't have missed for the world. I'm going to talk about a few of them here, and use the opportunity to illustrate how you might, if you are so inclined, do something similar.

Magazines

One day, a couple of years ago, I received an instant message from the editor of one of my favorite periodicals, *Haunted Magazine.* He was aware of my books, and would I be interested in putting together an article for the next issue?

That sounded fine and dandy to me, with just one small exception — they weren't paying anything.

I had always believed in the oft-quoted idea that money should always flow from the market to the writer, and that writing for free was a bad idea. I thought that it cheapened my attempts to become a professional writer, by giving away my valuable time in exchange for nothing.

Well, I say 'nothing,' but there was always the exposure that such an article would generate, I supposed. Then again, as my friend, the former U.S. Marine, master illusionist, and all-around nice guy Aiden Sinclair pointed out to me, "You're a paramedic. You of all people should know that people die of exposure."

I declined the gracious offer to write for *Haunted Magazine,* but after giving the matter a little more thought, I decided to get down off my high horse and recant. Yes, I would be writing for free, but it would give me an opportunity to write about something that I loved — more ghosts! — and reach a wider audience into the bargain.

The editor liked my story enough to offer a regular column, to be called 'The Step by Estep Guide to the Paranormal," which I thought was pretty punny. At the time of writing, I'm still putting out the column each issue, covering some of the haunted locations that I investigate and write books about.

The team at *Haunted* have been good to me, and have since become firm friends. They make a point of promoting my books whenever they can, to the point of giving me free ad space in the most recent issue.

There is also a paid market for freelance magazine writing, but, by all accounts it is a rather cutthroat business, with many freelancers vying for relatively few spots. Neither are those spots particularly well paid.

Depending upon the nature of your book and area of expertise, it may be possible for you to parlay your writing skills in exchange for an article, a column, and some free publicity.

Adventures on the Small Screen

"We're getting ready to the hero shot now. Okay, Richard. Stand still, and on three, walk toward the camera. *Be confident!* Keep your eyes on the lens. Go past the camera and sit down in the chair. Got all that?"

"I think so," I said, hoping that my nervousness wouldn't show up in the final cut.

"Good." The director relaxed back in her chair, and called, *"ACTION!"*

Doing my best to remember everything that she had asked me to do, I made my way slowly but (I hoped) confidently down the long, dark hallway toward the camera, backlit by a big industrial-sized light shining through a pair of frosted glass doors.

We were inside an old, abandoned school in the city of Toronto. It was pitch black outside, darkness having fallen quite a few hours ago, and the place was *freezing* cold...so much so, in fact, that the production manager had hired a jet heater. This thing roared like a turbine when it was running, venting heated air through a large-diameter hose that snaked from the outside of the building, up the stairs, and into the upstairs hallway where we were shooting season one of the TV show *Haunted Case Files*.

The premise of the show was simple: paranormal investigators from across the United States would share some of their most intense and disturbing experiences, recounting them during on-camera interviews. A few weeks afterward, the crew would go on to shoot dramatic reconstructions of those same cases. We, the investigators, would be played by actors. (When I saw the finished product, I was pleasantly surprised to find that the chap playing me in season one looked quite a bit like the actor Steve Carell, from TV's *The Office*).

We shot my segments of the show over the space of two

days. During breaks, I wandered around the school, poking into the dusty corners and closets. My aimless roaming turned up some truly bizarre findings, such as a large box of pornographic magazines hiding underneath one of the teacher's desks (therein must lay a tale, but I have *no* idea of what it could possibly be).

Several of the cases that we filmed in seasons one and two came from my books. The historic Callahan House was drawn from *Haunted Longmont*; Asylum 49, the former hospital now turned Halloween attraction, was featured in its own book, *The Haunting of Asylum 49*, co-written with Cami Andersen; my investigation into the haunting of 30 East Drive, home to what some claim was the world's most violent poltergeist, appeared in both *Trail of Terror* and *The Black Monk of Pontefract*; and the I-70 Strangler case received its own book, *The Horrors of Fox Hollow Farm*.

Having the subjects of those books appear on *Haunted Case Files* gave sales of those books a decent shot in the arm, and perhaps more importantly, introduced my work to an entirely new readership: the people who liked the show enough to Google me or the cases, found their way to the books I had written about them.

Contrary to what you might think, the pay for working on

TV shows like this ranges somewhere between poor and non-existent. Putting that aside, however, not only are they a lot of fun to shoot, but provide the writer with a level of publicity that could not be obtained by any other means.

I was on vacation in my native England, attending a science fiction convention on the south coast, when out of the blue I received an email from a Canadian TV company.

They were prepping a TV show to be called *Haunted Hospitals*. During the research process, they had come across my book, *The World's Most Haunted Hospitals*. As somebody with a medical background who also researched the subject of ghosts, would I be interested in appearing on the show as one of the resident experts?

What a complete no-brainer. Several months later, I was on a plane heading from Denver to Toronto once more. In my hand were a series of notes, given to me by the research department. Each document contained a single story, detailing the paranormal experiences of a healthcare worker or a patient in a hospital or nursing home. My job was to make notes on each case, and then provide an on-camera commentary, explaining some of the possible explanations for the creepy experiences, both paranormal and mundane.

We shot the show in a TV studio on the outskirts of the

city this time, not an ice cold, ramshackle old school. The public response to *Haunted Hospitals* has been extremely positive, and not only was it picked up for a second season, but also generated a spin-off show, *Paranormal 911,* which showcased the ghostly encounters of first responders.

P911, as I like to call it, was an even better fit for me than *Haunted Hospitals*. As a former firefighter and current paramedic by vocation, I speak the same language as the men and women who staff fire engines and ambulances. I like to think that I can speak intelligently about the differences between a psychiatric emergency and something a little more bizarre, a phenomenon which may have a paranormal explanation. Shooting *P911* was also a great experience, and a second season is currently due to go before the cameras next month. I'm thrilled to have been asked back to appear as an expert once again.

All being well, three weeks after we wrap on the second season of *P911,* I've been asked to contribute to a fourth TV show, this one titled *Paranormal Night Shift*. It will cover the terrifying experiences of those who work in various jobs from dusk til dawn, and once again, I'll be working as a subject matter expert (if there can actually be such a thing as an expert when it pertains to the paranormal!)

I owe all seven seasons of TV work — and hopefully more to come in the future — to a handful of the books I've written. One piece of good advice that was given to me in the past, I will now pass on to you: always say *yes* to an opportunity, no matter how odd it might seem at the time. This is also the philosophy of the ultimate 'working actor,' William Shatner, known for his roles in some truly great movies *and* some legendarily awful ones. Shatner remarks in his books and stage plays that he likes to take acting jobs because he never knows what doors will open because of them, and he's one hundred percent right. I never set out to be on TV, let alone make it a side career; I just said "Yes" when the chance arose.

The Texas-based paracon I attended, which ended up with me getting stiffed on the hotel room bill, led directly to me writing *The Fairfield Haunting*. I was livid at the time, but with the benefit of 20/20 hindsight, now I wouldn't have changed it for the world. I consider it to have been money very well spent, because without that particular stroke of bad luck, I may have missed out on a Gettysburg adventure that will stay with me forever.

If opportunity comes knocking, even if it arrives in the strangest of disguises, say yes. Speak at a library. Write a blog post for somebody, or the foreword for another author's book. Say yes to appearing on a pod cast if you're invited to. Sit on a panel at a convention. Say yes to book signings at a local book store, even if only two or three people attend.

You never know what's in store, if you're willing to work hard, keep an open mind, and say yes...

...and above all else, *keep writing*.

CHAPTER NINETEEN

Your Writing Journey

Thank you for sticking with me this far, for over 50,000 words of sometimes rambling prose, as I have attempted to share with you a roadmap to writing and publishing success.

As this book is going to press, it's 2019, with 2020 already peeking over the horizon at us. For the publishing industry, both traditional and independent, the future has never looked more uncertain. Although I'm reluctant to make too many predictions about how things are going to turn out, I feel very confident in saying that the traditional publishing houses will continue to lose market share to those of us who self-publish.

As far as I'm concerned, it isn't a competition. I enjoy being a hybrid author. I love my trad publishers and really appreciate the doors they have opened for me, particularly at the beginning of my writing career. I will probably continue to partner with them on a book every year or so, for as long as it makes sense for us both to do so. Yet the winds are changing, blowing ever more strongly in the direction of independent authors, who are increasingly reluctant to accept royalties of 7%, 10%, or even 25% when KDP is offering three times that amount.

Who can really blame them?

For you, dear reader (and fellow writer), as you start out on your publishing journey, determining which direction to take will probably be the toughest challenge. Once that decision has been made, you're well on the road to realizing your dream of becoming a published writer.

Now that we have come to the end of *Building the Write Life*, I encourage you to set the book aside for a while, and take some time to think about the questions I posed early on in the book.

In which subject area do you want to write? Fiction or non-fiction?

Do your research. Visit a bookstore and browse the appropriate shelves. Do the same thing online. Peruse Amazon's categories and subcategories. Check out their top 100 lists.

Then, once you have a clear direction in which to go, start writing.

And don't stop until you hit the end.

Resistance can't beat you. Inertia can't beat you. A bad first draft can't beat you.

Unless you let them.

Get to the end, come hell or high water. Then edit, edit, edit.

This time next year — or possibly even sooner — there can be a book sitting on the shelves with your name on it, and that, my friend, is a beautiful thing.

You've got this. You can do it. I *know* you can.

So what are you waiting for?

Get after it.

AFTERWORD

And so, dear reader, here we are. The end of the book. Counting the various pen names that I use, this is the twenty-fourth book I have completed during my lifetime, and believe me when I tell you that it was just as daunting an experience as writing the first twenty-three.

My great hope is that you will have been sufficiently inspired by this book to sit down and write your own. Nothing would give me greater pleasure than to know that my advice has been helpful in starting you down the path to publishing a book of your own. Do please drop me a line at richard@richardestep.net and tell me your own personal success story.

If you have indeed found this book to be helpful, please consider leaving a rating or a review at Amazon.com. That act of kindness would be greatly appreciated.

Very best wishes,
Richard Estep

www.ingramcontent.com/pod-product-compliance
Lightning Source LLC
Chambersburg PA
CBHW070617220526
45466CB00001B/36